FOOTPATHS FOR FITNESS

NORTHAMPTONSHIRE

FOOTPATHS FOR FITNESS

NORTHAMPTONSHIRE

Judith &
Ron Smith

COUNTRYSIDE BOOKS

NEWBURY BERKSHIRE

First published 2010
© Judith & Ron Smith 2010

All rights reserved. No reproduction
permitted without the prior permission
of the publisher:

COUNTRYSIDE BOOKS
3 Catherine Road
Newbury, Berkshire

To view our complete range of books,
please visit us at
www.countrysidebooks.co.uk

ISBN: 978 1 84674 182 1

Photographs by Ron Smith
Maps by CJWT Solutions

Designed by Peter Davies, Nautilus Design
Produced through MRM Associates Ltd., Reading
Typeset by CJWT Solutions, St Helens
Printed in Thailand

CONTENTS

FOOTPATHS FOR FITNESS

FOOTPATHS FOR FITNESS

GRADE 3 – HIKE

Introduction

The aim of this book is to encourage more people to take up walking as a pastime. We have put together 20 walks, differing in length and scattered throughout Northamptonshire, with the intention of giving you pleasant surroundings in which to enjoy your exercise.

Each of these walks is graded in an incremental fitness range of 1 to 3 according to length (they vary from 1 mile to 7½ miles) and gradient difficulty, 1 classifying the least taxing routes and 3 the most strenuous. To aid walk selection, the routes are grouped and the grading analysis is as follows:

Grade 1 – STROLL

Grade 2 – STRIDE

Grade 3 – HIKE

It has been said that walking is the nearest activity to perfect exercise, whether you want to improve your general health, keep fit, control your weight or perhaps regain your strength after an illness. All age groups can take part and walking can fit in with any lifestyle or economic circumstances.

Any walker will tell you that it is best to be correctly equipped. Footwear should be laced and can be trainers, proper walking shoes or boots, according to the terrain. Bare legs are not a good idea. Lightweight rainwear can be bought at reasonable prices, some in packs which can be attached to a belt. Hats and sun cream to protect against the elements are a personal choice. On longer walks, take water and energy snacks. Switch off that mobile phone and only use it in an emergency!

For general health, experts recommend 30 minutes of brisk walking each day. Brisk means fast without over exertion, i.e. when you can just about hold a conversation at the same time. Walk away from your home for 15 minutes, then return feeling so much better! Parking further from the school, office or station adds a few more steps. There is always the gym as an alternative, but this cannot provide the stimulus that is to be found in the countryside – which costs nothing!

Help the kids get the active habit by treating the walk as an adventure. Go at their pace and have a landmark to aim for such as a tall tree or a stile in the distance to make it fun. The odd healthy snack goes down well, too.

The Welland viaduct, a well-known Northamptonshire landmark

Our towns are full of parks and there are often country parks on the outskirts, too.

Northamptonshire is a great county for walking and we have devised a variety of routes from Deene in the north to Cosgrove in the south; from short walks like the one at Salcey Forest to the more challenging hike at King's Cliffe. So, go and explore our beautiful county on foot and reap the benefits!

Judith and Ron Smith

Publisher's Note

We hope that you obtain considerable enjoyment from this book; great care has been taken in its preparation. Although at the time of publication all routes followed public rights of way or permitted paths, diversion orders can be made and permissions withdrawn.

We cannot, of course, be held responsible for such diversion orders and any inaccuracies in the text which result from these or any other changes to the routes, nor any damage which might result from walkers trespassing on private property. We are anxious though that all details covering the walks are kept up to date and would therefore welcome information from readers which would be relevant to future editions.

The simple sketch maps that accompany the walks in this book are based on notes made by the authors whilst checking out the routes on the ground. They are designed to show you how to reach the start, to point out the main features of the overall circuit and they contain a progression of numbers that relate to the paragraphs of the text.

However, for the benefit of a proper map, we do recommend that you purchase the relevant Ordnance Survey sheet covering your walk. The Ordnance Survey maps are widely available, especially through booksellers and local newsagents.

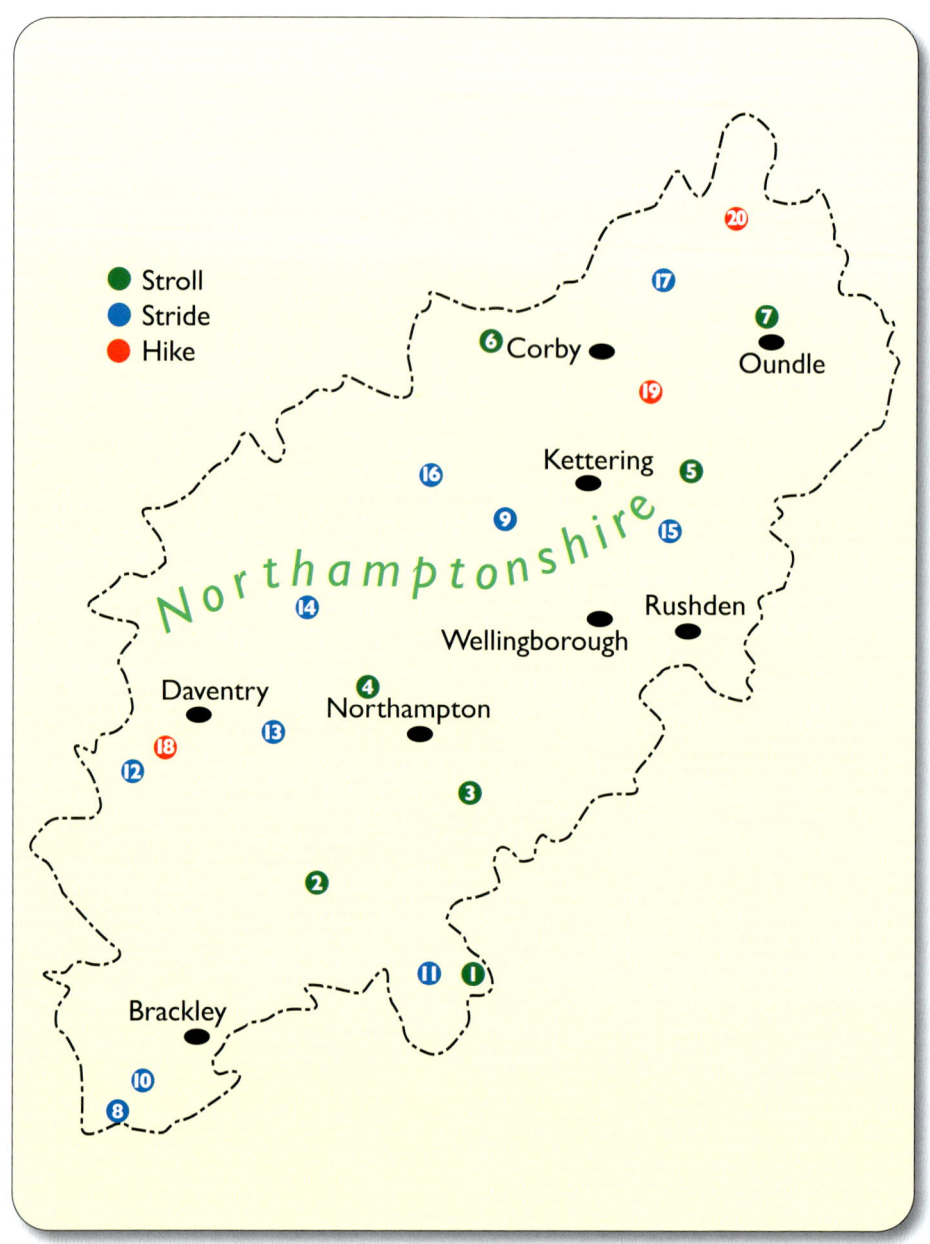

Area map showing locations of the walks

1 Cosgrove

Away from the Crowds

FOOTPATHS
FOR FITNESS

■ *The ornamental bridge over the canal* ■

Cosgrove lies not far from the hustle and bustle of the Milton Keynes Shopping Centre. Here, though, you can escape from it all and enjoy a tranquil walk along part of the Grand Union Canal. This waterway was busy in the 18th and 19th centuries transporting coal and heavy goods but these days is used for pleasure. Take a look at Cosgrove's 15th-century church before you set off on your walk and admire its timbered roof.

> ### GRADE: 1
> ### ESTIMATED CALORIE BURN: 300
>
> **Distance:** 2 miles
> **Time:** 50 minutes
> **Stiles:** 1
> **Terrain:** Mainly level walking, with a slight pull in the middle but nothing very strenuous.
> **Map:** OS Explorer 207 Newport Pagnell & Northampton South
> **Starting point:** The car park near the Barley Mow pub. GR 792425
> **How to get there:** Cosgrove is approximately 8 miles south-east of Towcester. Taking the A5 south from Towcester, turn onto the A508 at a roundabout just north of Old Stratford following signs to Cosgrove. Follow the road into the village and turn right before the no through road. The car park is on the left.
> **Refreshments:** The Barley Mow in Cosgrove. Telephone: 01908 562957.

1 Leave the car park going left downhill and follow the road to an unusual horse tunnel going underneath the ***Grand Union Canal***. On emerging, turn sharp right up a flight of steps onto the canal towpath. Turn right and soon a very pretty Gothic-style bridge comes into view. Built in the 1790s, at the insistence of the Biggins family who were local landowners, it is one of only two ornamental bridges over the canal. To continue along the towpath go up to the road, cross the bridge and descend to the path again. This is a tranquil stretch of the canal with views over to the right of **Castlethorpe church**. Here there is plenty of opportunity to put a spring in your step! Soon the taverner's private moorings come into view and shortly afterwards a bridge where you leave the canal.

2 Turn left uphill in front of the **Navigation Inn**. It is a bit of a pull up here but not for long. Pass the bridleway sign on the right and carry on uphill for about 150 yards to another bridleway sign hidden in the hedge on the left. Go through the gate and continue along through a series of gates as indicated by the waymarker signs. When houses are reached, continue along the back of the gardens on the path with hedges on either side. Meet the road at the end and turn left to walk back to the ornamental bridge. Cross it and descend to the towpath retracing your steps to the start.

There is much more to be seen in this area. If you are happy to walk south along the canal, you can view the 'Iron Trunk' aqueduct which was built to

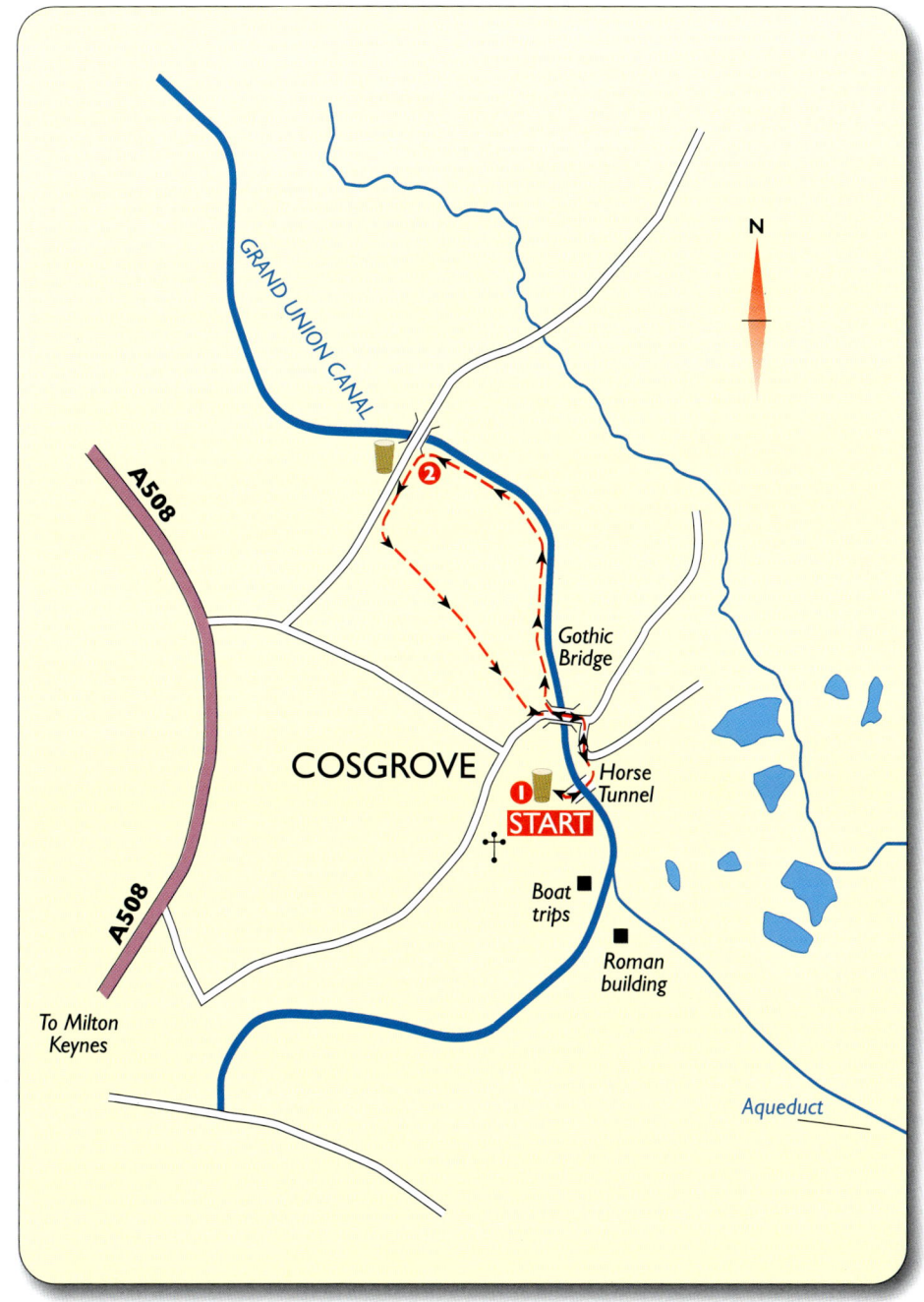

GRAND UNION CANAL

A508

A508

N

②

Gothic
Bridge

COSGROVE

Horse
Tunnel

①
START

Boat
trips

Roman
building

To Milton
Keynes

Aqueduct

■ *The horse tunnel in Cosgrove* ■

replace the original brick aqueduct constructed in 1805 to take the canal across the valley without the need for a large number of locks. However, the brick aqueduct collapsed only three years later and temporary locks had to be used until the iron one was put in place in 1881.

2 Greens Norton

A Royal Retreat

FOOTPATHS FOR FITNESS

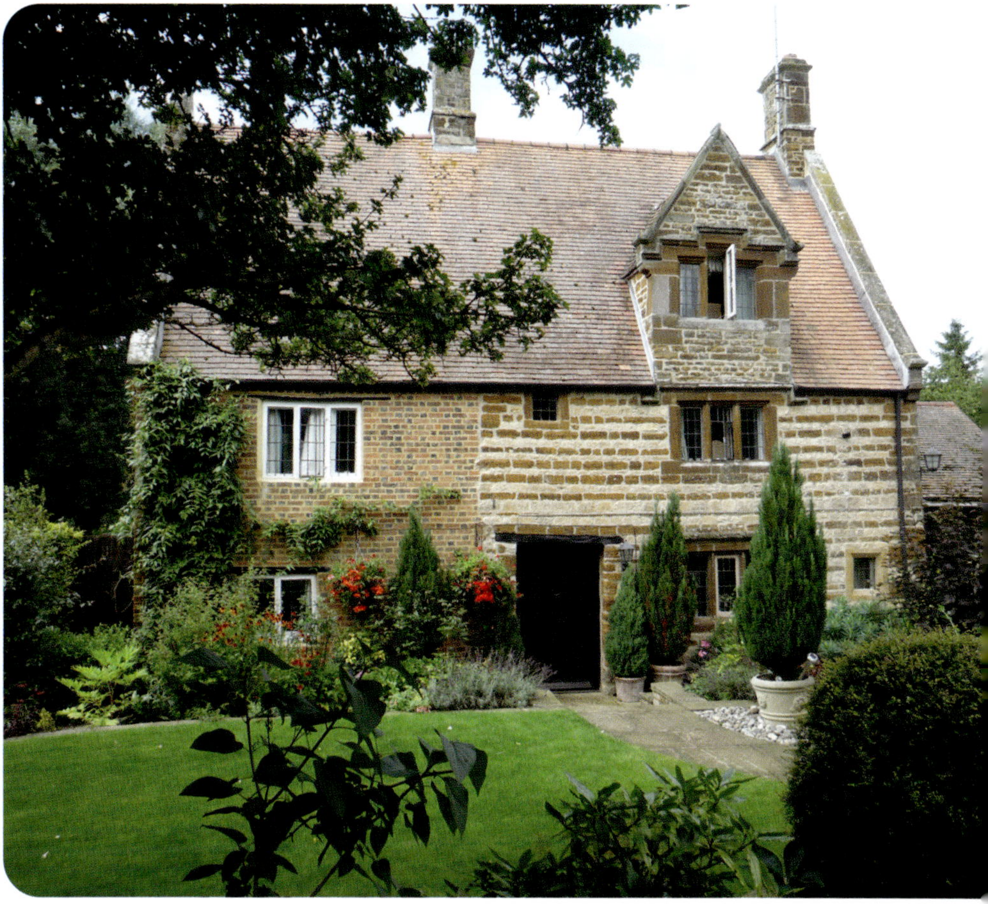

■ *Birds House, the oldest in the village* ■

Greens Norton is an interesting village with a royal connection. The Greene family owned the manor up until 1506. Two daughters were left, one of whom became the mother of Catherine Parr, widow of Henry VIII. The walk winds its way through the village, out into the fields to the south and then returns via the northern end of the village.

> **GRADE: 1**
> **ESTIMATED CALORIE BURN: 260**
>
> **Distance:** 1½ miles
> **Time:** 45 minutes
> **Stiles:** 1
> **Terrain:** Easy walking on level ground
> **Map:** OS Explorer 207 Newport Pagnell & Northampton South
> **Starting point:** The village green. GR 668498
> **How to get there:** Greens Norton is just north-west of Towcester and is well signed west of where the A5 and A43 meet at a roundabout. On entering the village, turn left in front of the Butcher's Arms to arrive at the green.
> **Refreshments:** The Butcher's Arms in Greens Norton. Telephone: 01327 350488.

1 Leave the green, walking up **Bradden Road** and turn left at the footpath and **Pocket Park** sign opposite the Methodist chapel. Cross the road and join the next section of the footpath. At the end go through the kissing gate, climb the stile on the left and head diagonally left across the field to another kissing gate. Turn left here along the path running beside a garden. Emerge onto **Bengal Lane** and turn right. On the right is a stone cottage called **The Maltings** where beer was brewed in the 1800s. Further along, before the road turns right, is a stone and brick cottage known as **Birds House**. This is the oldest house in the village and is reputed to have been lived in by Catherine Parr, Henry VIII's sixth wife.

2 Where the road swings right you will see a bridleway leading off to the left. Go through the gate and follow the track alongside the wall of **Greens Norton Hall**. The route can be a bit muddy here at times. Proceed through the wooden gate at the end and keep beside the metal fence running parallel with the drive which is bordered by some large pines and holly bushes. Leave the field via a white gate and, with great care, cross the road and follow the footpath sign into the field.

3 Walk on for approximately 80 yards to an intersection of paths at which point turn left onto the **Grafton Way** (though at this point there is no mention of it) heading in the direction of the church and a gap in the

hedge with a gate. From here, go straight ahead through housing and emerge onto the main road along **Church View**, a road with houses on either side.

Turn left to the village, turning left again in front of the **Butcher's Arms** to arrive back at the green.

■ *Every which way!* ■

Used in medieval times as a royal hunting ground the ancient woodland of Salcey Forest is a wonderful place for walking. Beautiful trees abound, including oaks thought to be 500 years old. Today the woodland is carefully tended by the Forestry Commission and made available as a leisure area. Within it are well-marked trails of differing lengths for walkers, cyclists, and horse riders. The wooden Treetop Walk which rises above the tree canopy is very special. Salcey Forest is a popular spot especially at weekends and holiday times when it can get busy.

1 Before setting out on the trail and to add enjoyment to the walk, head towards some information boards, near the café, where you can read some interesting facts about the forest, as well as look at a beautifully illustrated board showing what can be seen in terms of flora and fauna in any given month. Proceed towards a large wooden colour-coded post beside the children's play area. The trail chosen for this circuit is the **Elephant Walk** with a detour to the **Treetop Walk** which is marked in purple. Carry on round to the left of the play area to start the walk. The paths are flat and give a good chance to walk at a brisk pace whilst still enjoying the delights of the woodland. Seats appear from time to time but try to ignore them!

2 After a time, a track comes in from the left with two signs saying 'No cycling please'. Turn left here (the sign could be easily missed). Continue on,

GRADE: 1
ESTIMATED CALORIE BURN: 200

Distance: 1 mile
Time: 30 minutes
Stiles: 0
Terrain: Level on sound paths. There is a bit of a climb up to the wooden Treetop Walk but it is well worth the effort.
Map: OS Explorer 207 Newport Pagnell & Northampton South
Starting point: The car park in the forest (fee payable). GR 795515
How to get there: Salcey Forest lies between the villages of Quinton and Hanslope, 6 miles south-east of Northampton. The entrance is well signed.
Refreshments: The Forest Café beside the car park. (Note: they only accept cash or cheques.)

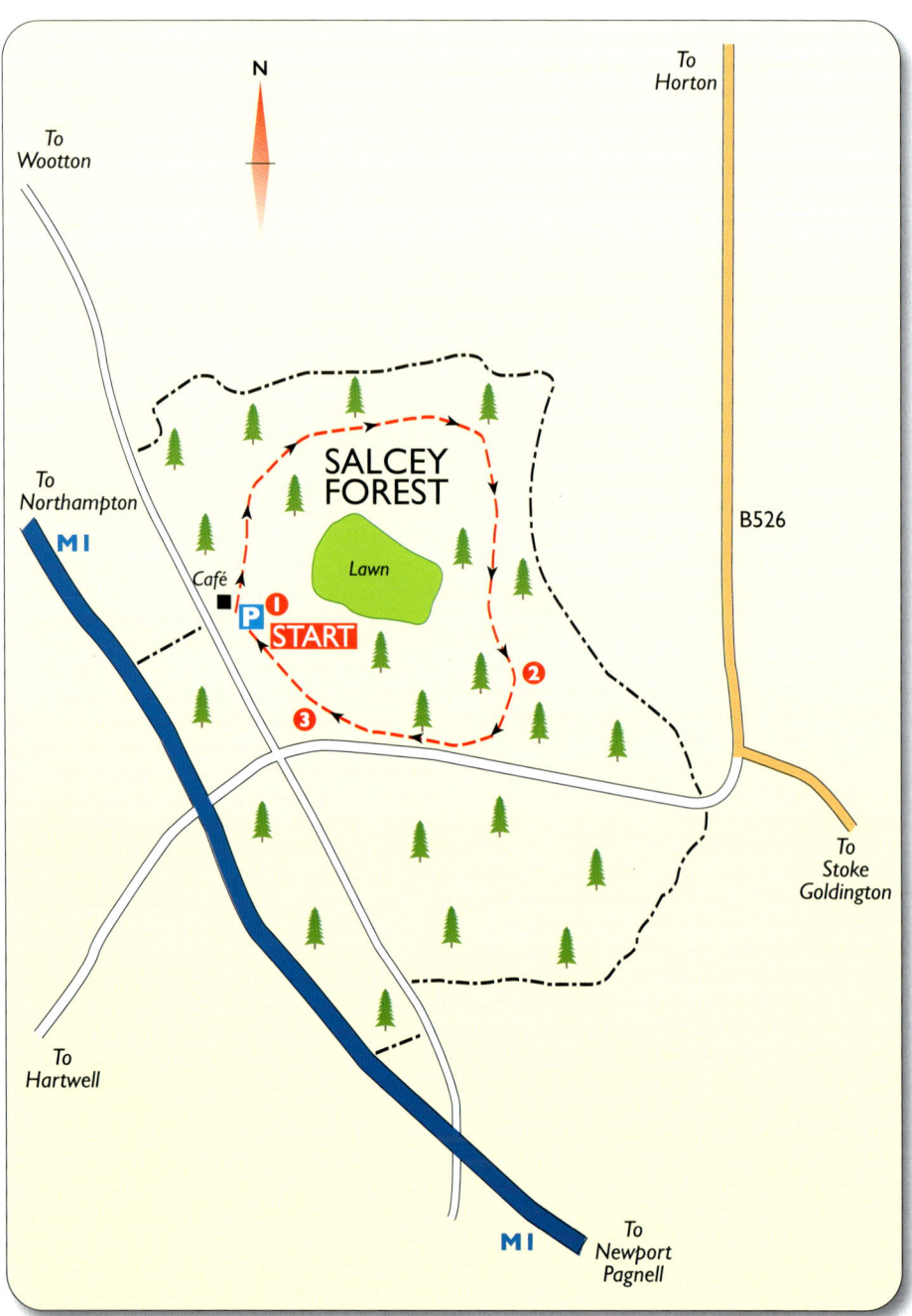

■ *The Treetop Walk* ■

ignoring a wooden walkway on the **Woodpecker trail** going left, and head for the sign to the **Elephant Walk** and **Treetop Walk** which is over the road.

3 At a small clearing with a lone picnic table, turn left onto a wooden suspension bridge over the 'elephant pond'. At the end of it, you will see the start of the **Treetop Walk**, as well as a stone monument with a plaque commemorating the countryside award presented by the Duke of Edinburgh in 1970. The gradient of this walkway is 1 in 12, so it's not too taxing. If you have a head for heights you will be well rewarded at the top with views of the surrounding area and the thought that you have given your heart muscle a bit of a workout as well. Return to the picnic table and carry on admiring the woodland and listening to the birds as you follow the purple signs back to the start. Your walk was 1 mile. How about setting off again on the **Woodpecker trail**? Keep the 6-mile walk up your sleeve for when your level of fitness improves!

4 Harlestone

A Woodland Wander

■ *The start of the walk* ■

These **large woodlands are owned** by the Althorpe Estate and are managed for the production of timber. There are designated footpaths and bridleways and, with the permission of the Estate, one may roam on the many paths within the woodland. Most of the trees are fir but many other species have been planted. This is a lovely peaceful place in which to walk and keep up a good pace, while the odd jogger passing by gives you an incentive to rev up a bit! There are endless tracks to follow and plenty of wildlife to spot. In spring the bluebells are a sight to behold.

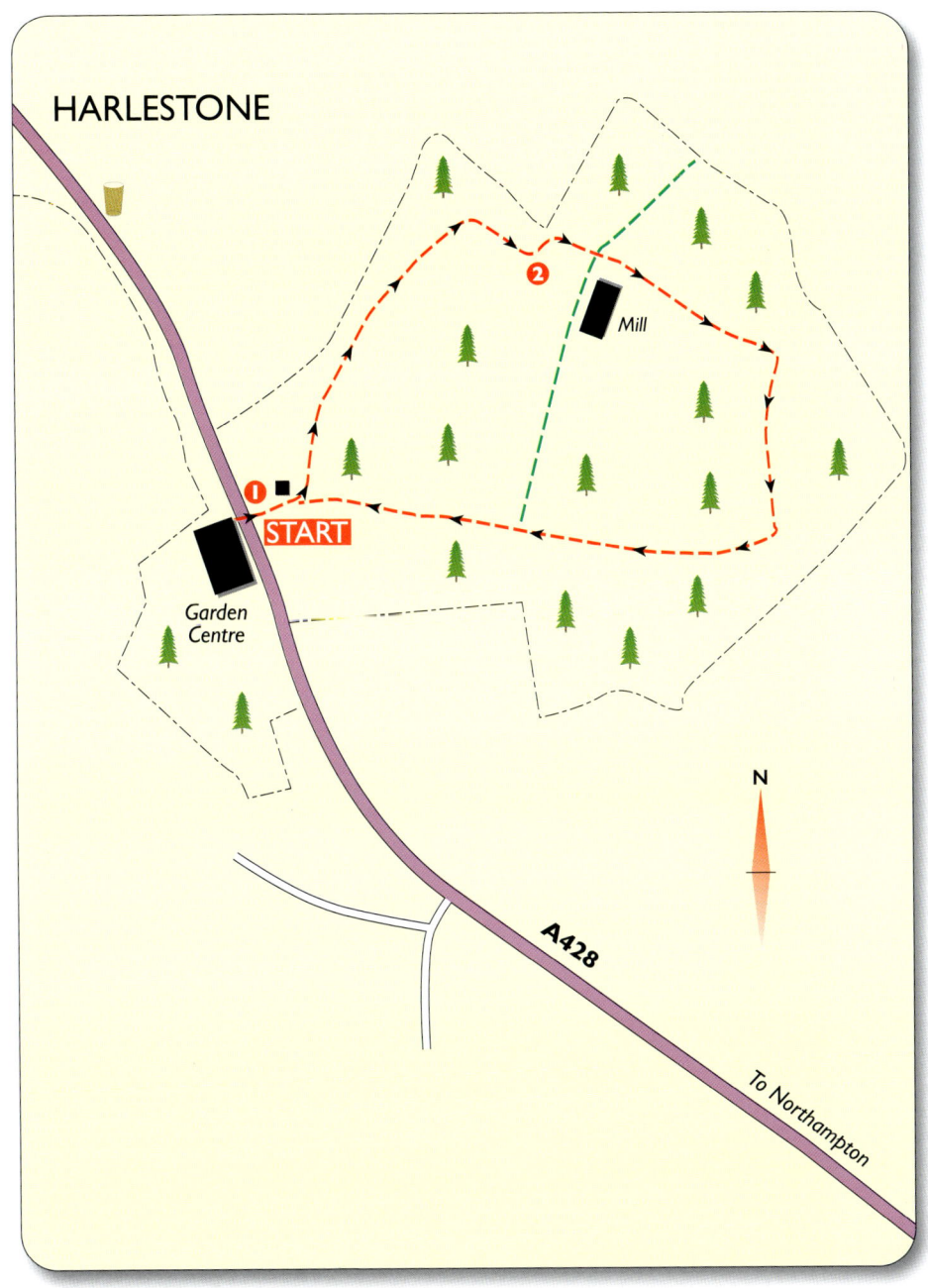

HARLESTONE

Mill

START

Garden
Centre

N

A428

To Northampton

GRADE: 1
ESTIMATED CALORIE BURN: 300

Distance: 2 miles
Time: 30 minutes
Stiles: 0
Terrain: Flat on woodland paths and tracks
Map: OS Explorer 223 Northampton & Market Harborough
Starting point: The large lay-by outside the Harlestone Firs Garden Centre. GR 712637
How to get there: Take the A428 road north-west out of Northampton on the Harlestone road. The Harlestone Firs Garden Centre is on the left.
Refreshments: The garden centre has a café; alternatively the Fox and Hounds pub (telephone: 01604 821251) is a short way to the north on the A428.

1 Cross the road with great care, (traffic along this stretch of road travels at deceptively fast speeds), and go into the wood by the HFS timber entrance. Only vehicles visiting the sawmill are allowed access. Turn left immediately on the bridleway into the woodland and continue along the track. If you are feeling adventurous, you could at some stage explore some of the many paths to the left or right. The path becomes a wide grassy way, with a lot of new planting of trees such as oak and birch. Where the track curves round to the right, take the track coming in from the left and, after about 100 yards, turn right onto a public bridleway, the sign being on the left by a corner of an open field.

2 Go straight ahead at the next intersection and you will glimpse the sawmill over to the right. At the next intersection by a triangle of trees, turn right going slightly uphill, noticing on the right a new plantation of trees beside this wide track. At the next junction turn right and arrive at the entrance to the timber yard on the right. Turn left down a concrete road. There is a wide open area on the left. Keep on the road as it veers round to the right. This could be an opportunity to finish with a flourish by upping the pace and deserving that low-calorie drink! After a short while the entrance to the woodland can be seen in the distance.

Quiet tracks abound

5 Twywell Hills and Dales

Take Your Pick

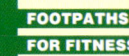

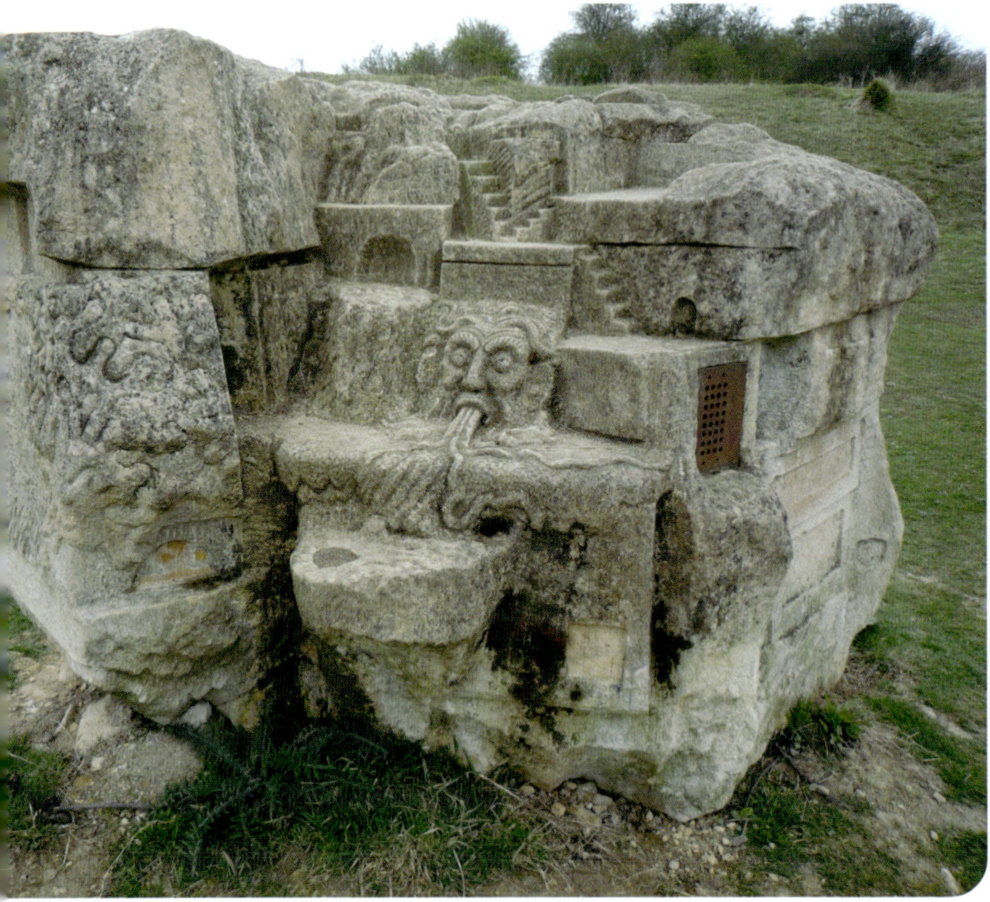

■ *The carved limestone boulder seen on the route* ■

This area was once grassy pasture but quarrying in 1928 turned it into what it is today. Following extensive quarrying for iron ore, the area was allowed to revert to nature and is now a Site of Special Scientific Interest watched over by wildlife trusts. There are rare species of ants, butterflies and sheep; and a pond is home to a colony of great crested newts.

Whitestones, where this walk is located, is so-called because of the white limestone underlying the grass. This is really a 'pick and mix' walk as there are many trails to follow once your level of fitness rises. The route winds its way among the hills and hollows so you encounter few steep slopes and can go at a steady pace.

1 Leave the back of the car park and head left to a wooden gate. Go through the gate and, after reading the information board, turn left and within a short distance turn right up a gentle gradient indicated by a green arrow, noticing the deep railway cutting on the left. Carry on towards a large lump of limestone carved with all sorts of interesting imagery.

2 Turn sharp left and climb a flight of steps, then just maybe, make use of the bench a little further on near an information board. Continue past the next seat, bear right and then left beside the pond. The path goes straight on towards an intersection, at which point go ahead to the hedge and bear right down a path which can be a bit boggy. Meet a fingerpost at the end indicating routes you could take on another visit.

3 Now turn back and go left in the direction of the green arrow. Ignore the next green arrow and go ahead with the wind farm on the horizon. Bear left at the end towards a wooden gate but do not go through it. Instead,

GRADE: 1
ESTIMATED CALORIE BURN: 230

Distance: 1¼ miles
Time: 45 minutes
Stiles: 0
Terrain: Humps and hollows rather than hills and dales! Mostly on grassy tracks.
Map: OS Explorer 224 Corby, Kettering & Wellingborough
Starting point: The car park in the Hills and Dales Country Park. GR 938772
How to get there: Turn off the A14 at junction 11 and follow signs to Cranford. Very quickly a large brown sign points right into the park.
Refreshments: The Red Lion in Cranford St John. Telephone: 01536 330724.

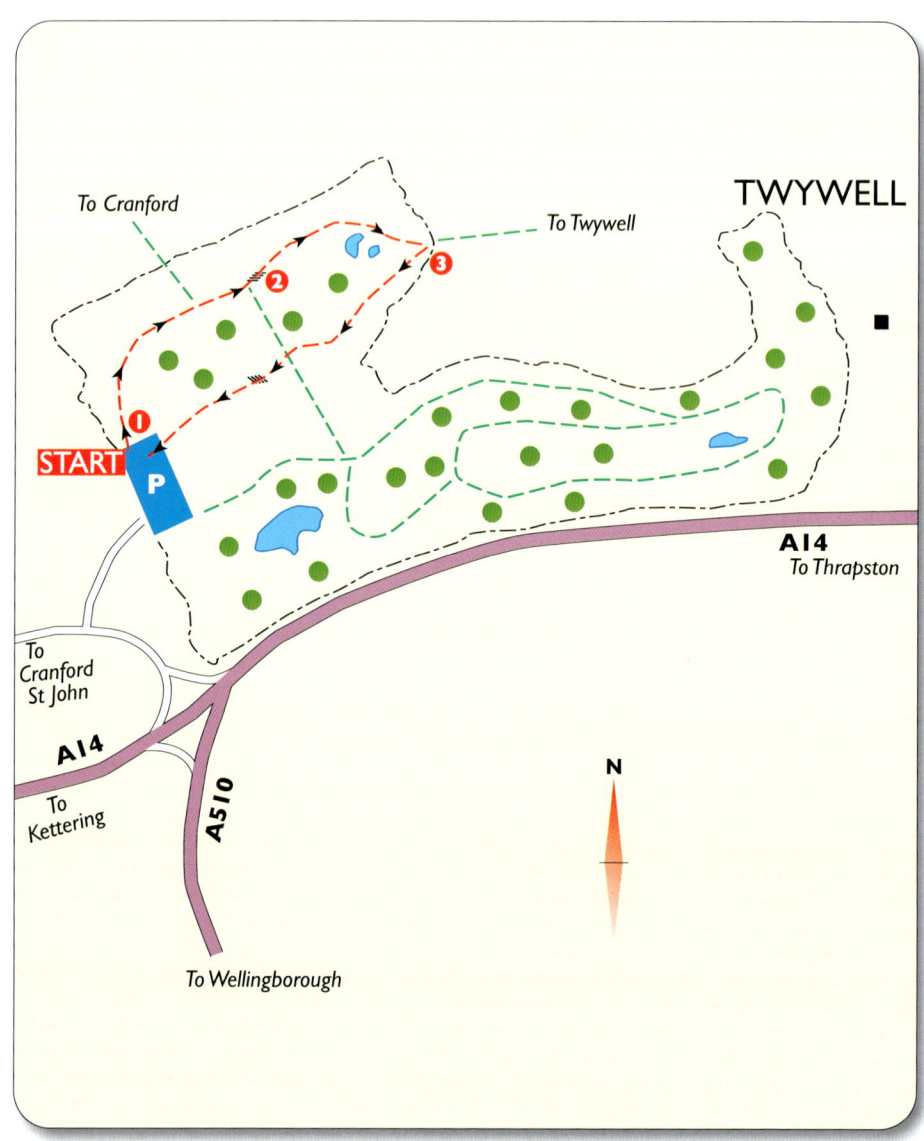

keep the wire fence on your left and walk down the slope passing a farm gate and ascend the mound in front. Carry on down a narrower track bordered by hawthorn hedges and after going down the steps, turn left towards a great deal of woodwork! Go through two gates, turn right and return to the car park.

6 East Carlton

A Tree Lover's Delight

FOOTPATHS FOR FITNESS

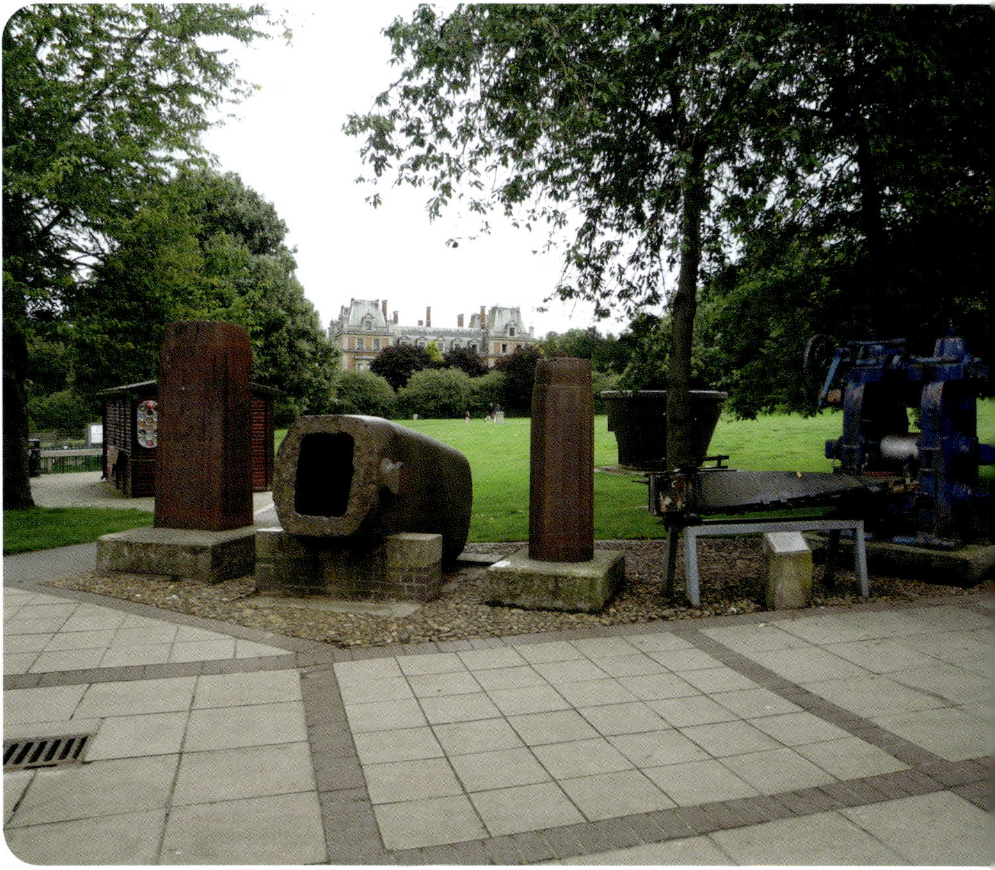

■ *The Steel Works artefacts on display near the car park* ■

This walk is in East Carlton Country Park which sits on the edge of the Welland Valley. The park is, in fact, the grounds of an imposing mansion built in 1863, but not open to the public. The offices of the former Stewarts and Lloyds, steel tube manufacturers of Corby, were housed there during the Second World War. The company supplied the pipeline, known as Pluto which went under the sea to supply the invading forces following the D-Day landings.

Distance: 1¼ miles
Time: 40 minutes
Stiles: 0
Terrain: Just a few gentle slopes and mainly on firm ground.
Map: OS Explorer 224 Corby, Kettering & Wellingborough
Starting point: The car park as you enter the country park. GR 834894
How to get there: East Carlton Country Park is well signed off the A427 between Corby and Market Harborough, approximately 4 miles west of Corby.
Refreshments: The café in the Heritage Centre. Telephone: 01536 770977.

There are some wonderful trees in the park, among them a lime with what is reputed to have the largest bole in Britain. An information board shows the trails which can be followed but the signs in the park are a bit unreliable. There is a heritage centre in the converted coach house and the stables are occupied by a craft workshop, a doll's house shop which children will love and a café. A most interesting display depicts the history of Corby and the growth of the iron and steel industry. The park closes at 8 pm in the summer and 4 pm in winter.

1 Leave the car park and head for the **Heritage Centre** passing on your way some very large artefacts from the steel works and an information board. Continue past the café in the direction of the nature trail signed on the fingerpost and down onto an obvious path noticing the hall over to the right. At the second wooden seat turn left down the slope towards the trees where beneath them you will see a delightful pond full of ducks and a rather splendid silver galleon with the surrounding trees reflected in the water. Cross the wooden footbridge continuing round the pond and turn left before the next footbridge with a metal dragonfly in front of you. Carry on along the path ignoring the sharp turn up to the right and carry on down a small path into the woods. Stay on the main path ignoring various tracks off to the side. This is a fairly uphill path so keep a steady pace to give the heart some exercise. When you come to a clearing with a tree leaning over the path, turn left and then right in the direction of the arrow. After a while you will see a nature trail arrow which you follow in the woodland. Soon a

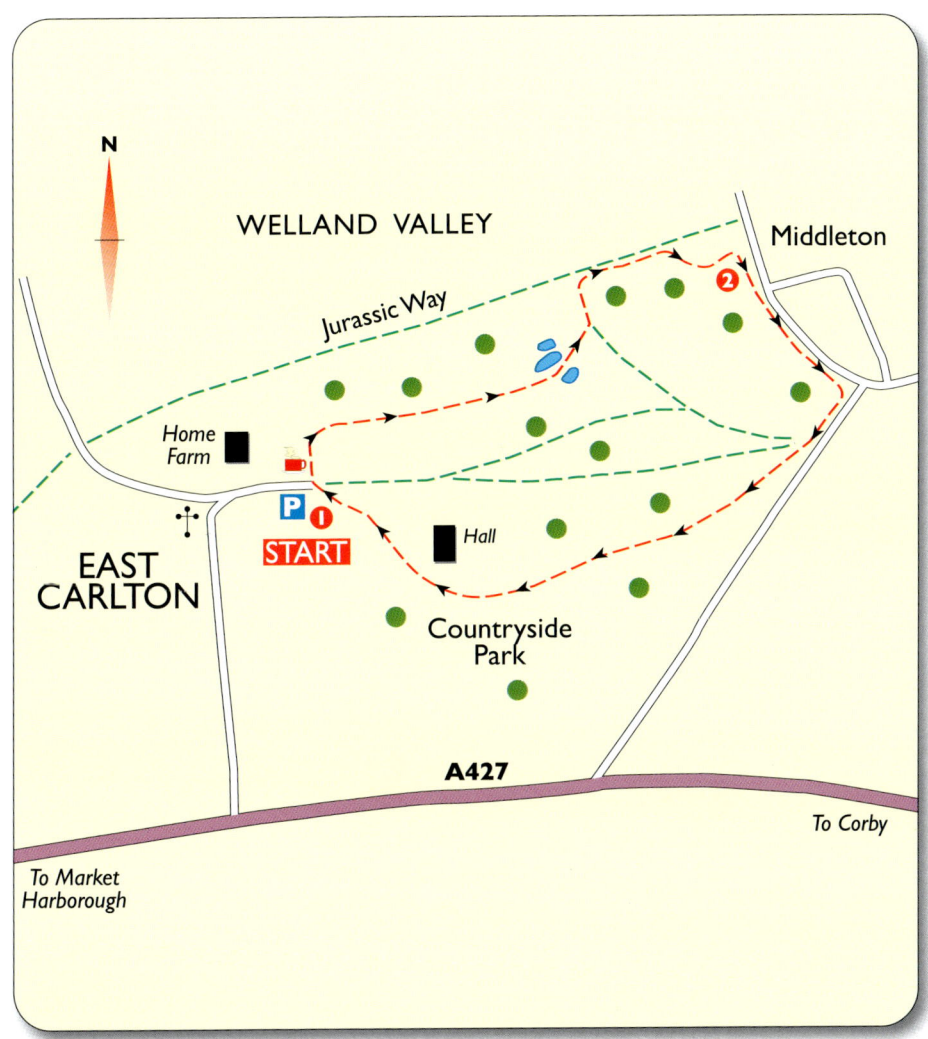

lovely view opens out of the **Welland Valley**. Seats are strategically placed but of course you will ignore them and keep walking, noticing the lovely beech trees as you go. Keep on the main path, maintaining a good speed, which goes up and round to the right.

2 A stone wall appears on the left, behind which is the road. Carry on following the nature trail keeping the wall on your left. Where the path descends there are some magnificent lime trees. If you are walking in

■ *Views of the Welland Valley* ■

late June, the scent is overpowering. A little further on, the wrought-iron gates of the mansion appear on the right. Carry on along the path to return to the car park. Although you are now back at the start, this need not be the end of your exercise; there are other areas which can be explored and volunteers are always needed to help with a spot of digging as you may have read!

7 Short Wood

Bluebells and Birdsong

FOOTPATHS FOR FITNESS

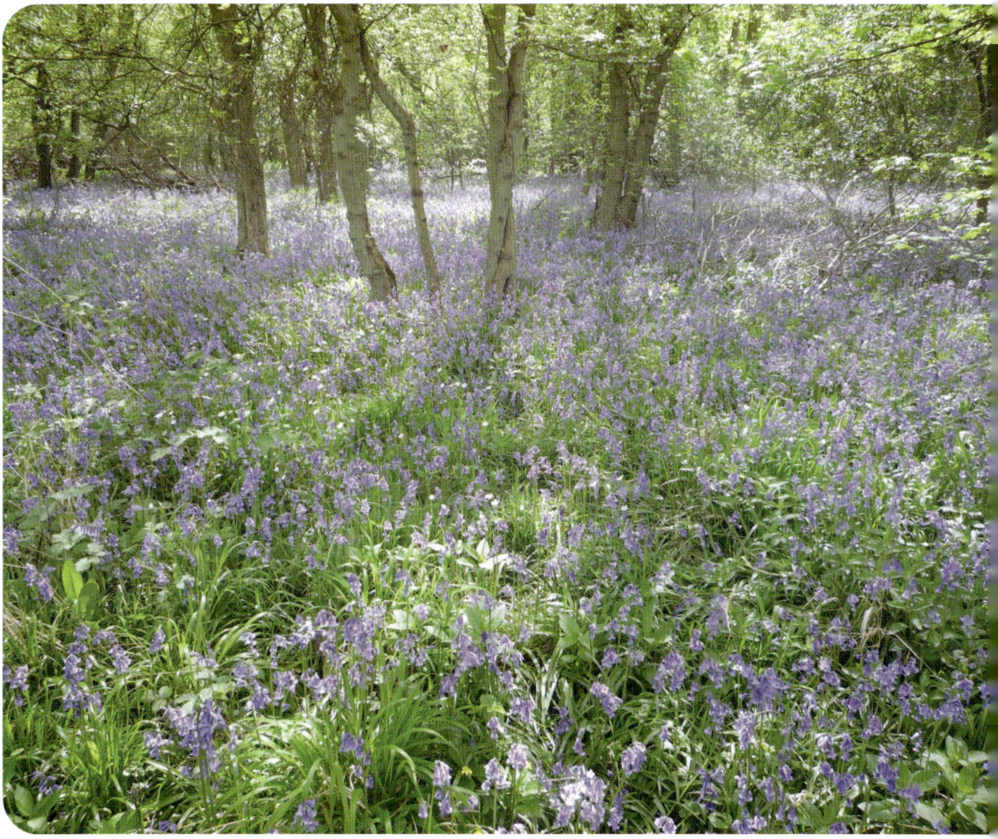

■ *Springtime in Short Wood* ■

This is a magical place at any time of year but more especially on a sunny May morning when the woodland floor is a carpet of bluebells as far as the eye can see. The reserve is owned and managed by the local Wildlife Trust who arrange occasional meetings in the wood at 4 am to hear the dawn chorus. Around 35 species of birds breed in the wood every year and will sing to you all the way round. On some evenings people gather in Glapthorn Cow Pasture, another reserve nearby, to hear the nightingales sing.

GRADE: 1
ESTIMATED CALORIE BURN: 260

Distance: 1½ miles
Time: 35 minutes
Stiles: 0
Terrain: Flat, on woodland paths.
Map: OS Explorer 224 Corby, Kettering & Wellingborough
Starting point: The lay-by beside the entrance to Short Wood. GR 024913
How to get there: From the centre of Oundle at the war memorial, take the road going north to Glapthorn and Southwick. Having passed Glapthorn, continue to the top of the hill and park in the lay-by on the left just short of the water tower.
Refreshments: The Shuckburgh Arms in nearby Southwick (not to be confused by a pub of the same name in neighbouring Stoke Doyle). Telephone: 01832 274007. The town of Oundle, of course, is full of coffee bars and pubs.

1 From the lay-by, follow the signpost marking the bridleway and the **Wildlife Nature Reserve**. Carry on along this wide track beside the hedge until the very obvious entrance to the wood appears. An information board tells you all about the flora and fauna you might see. The map shows two suggested trails although they are not marked on the actual route. The following guidelines will lead you round.

2 Go through the gate and take the path to the left. Go past **Jackson's Ride** on the left and, where the path curves round at **Burton's**, continue with the curve and carry on along the path. Just beyond where **Primrose Ride** comes in from the left, continue going slightly downhill but bear round to the right keeping the fence on your left. The entire wood is fenced to keep the large number of deer from entering.

3 Continue along the path until your exit gate is reached. This has been a short walk but, as you will have gathered, there are other paths to be explored adding to your enjoyment and increasing the level of exercise! Why not follow the track to **Glapthorn Cow Pastures** and back? These pastures, now a wood, were originally grazed by the cattle of the inhabitants of Glapthorn. The Brudenall family purchased the land and planted the trees to encourage birds for the shoot.

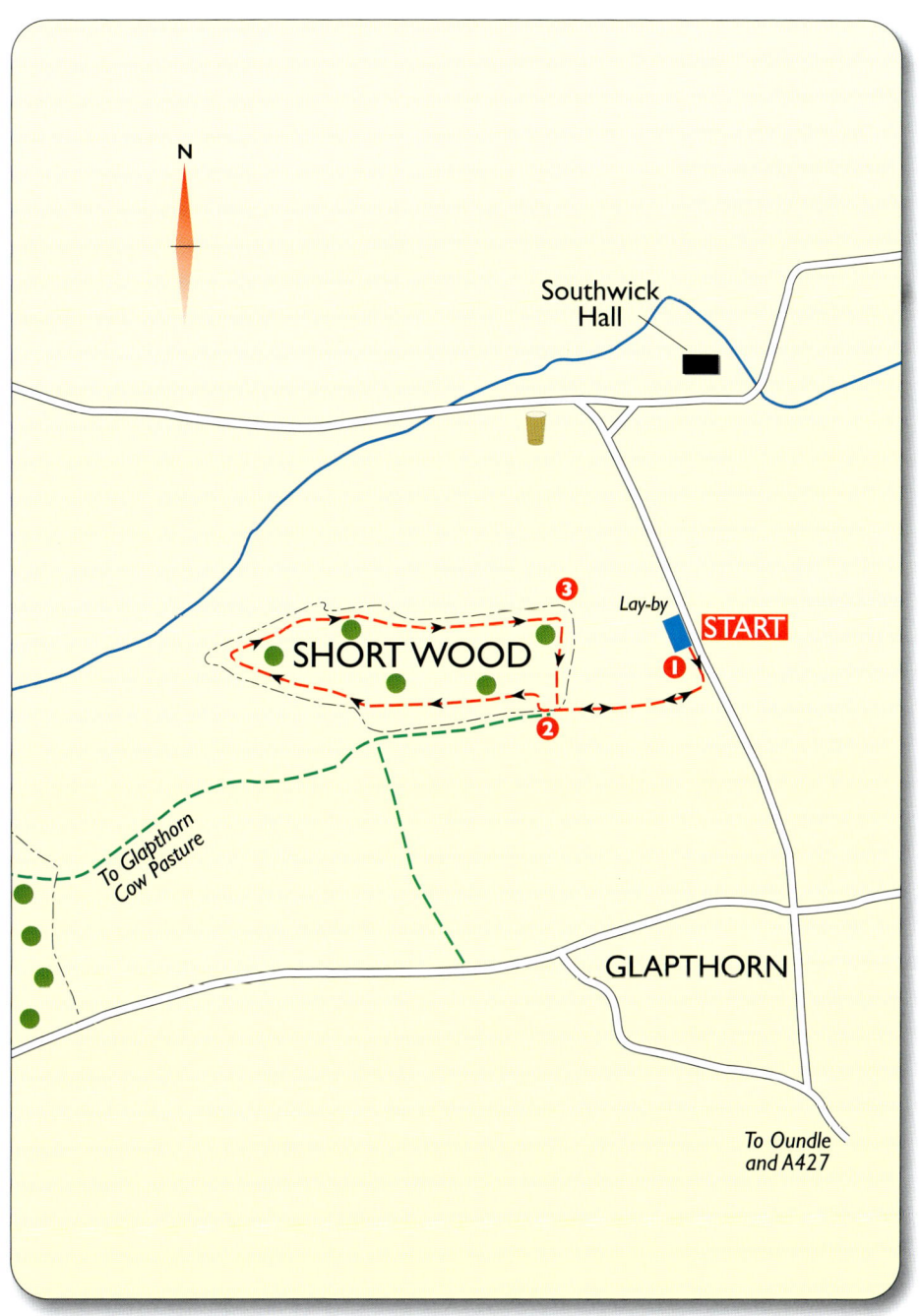

Stepping Out from the Apricot Village

Attractive apricot-clad stone cottages in Aynho

This pretty village with its thatched stone cottages is known as the Apricot Village, so-called because the houses along the main road are clad with apricot trees. Aynho House was once the home of the Cartwright family who had lived there since 1616. The house was virtually burned down during the English Civil War by the Royalists who took exception to the Parliamentary sympathies of the Cartwrights. Sadly, in 1954 the squire and his son were killed in a car crash and to pay the death duties the house was sold to the Country Houses Association who turned it into private apartments.

The walk takes you south of Aynho across the fields towards Souldern and returns beside the grounds of the house.

1 Walk back down **The Portway** to the main road. Cross it to a footpath sign and enter the lane over a stone stile. Walk on down the lane between the marvellous drystone walls. Climb the stile at the end and carry straight on downhill with open fields on either side and woodland ahead. Go through a kissing gate and diagonally left to a white disc beside a metal gate. Go through the kissing gate and proceed downhill on the concrete track and through the trees. Having crossed the **Ockley Brook** you are now in Oxfordshire and heading for a metal gate beside which is a stile. Climb it and walk up the field beside the fence. About 100 yards before you reach the conifers, you will see, on the right, the remains of an unmarked stile beside a sycamore tree which has been fenced. Climb over the stile. (Should you find this difficult, carry on along the fence and go through the gate.) Once in the field keep to the left of two conifers and head for the hedge on the left on the other side of some oak and sycamore trees (there is a farm gate in the hedge). Continue right, with the woodland on your left. Across to the right is a view of the imposing **Aynho House**. Go over the stile beside a metal gate then beside a metal fence, a stone wall and a house. To the left of the wooden

GRADE: 2
ESTIMATED CALORIE BURN: 460

Distance: 3 miles
Time: 1½ hours
Stiles: 6
Terrain: Mostly on field paths and tracks. Level walking apart from the final approach into Aynho.
Map: OS Explorer 191 Banbury, Bicester & Chipping Norton
Starting point: The Portway. GR 518334
How to get there: Turn west off the A43 south of Brackley onto the B4031 signed to Croughton and Aynho. On entering Aynho on the B4031, immediately after the 'gate', turn right into The Portway and park by the side of the road.
Refreshments: The Rose and Crown in nearby Charlton (telephone: 01869 811317) or the Cartwright Hotel in Aynho (telephone: 01869 811885).

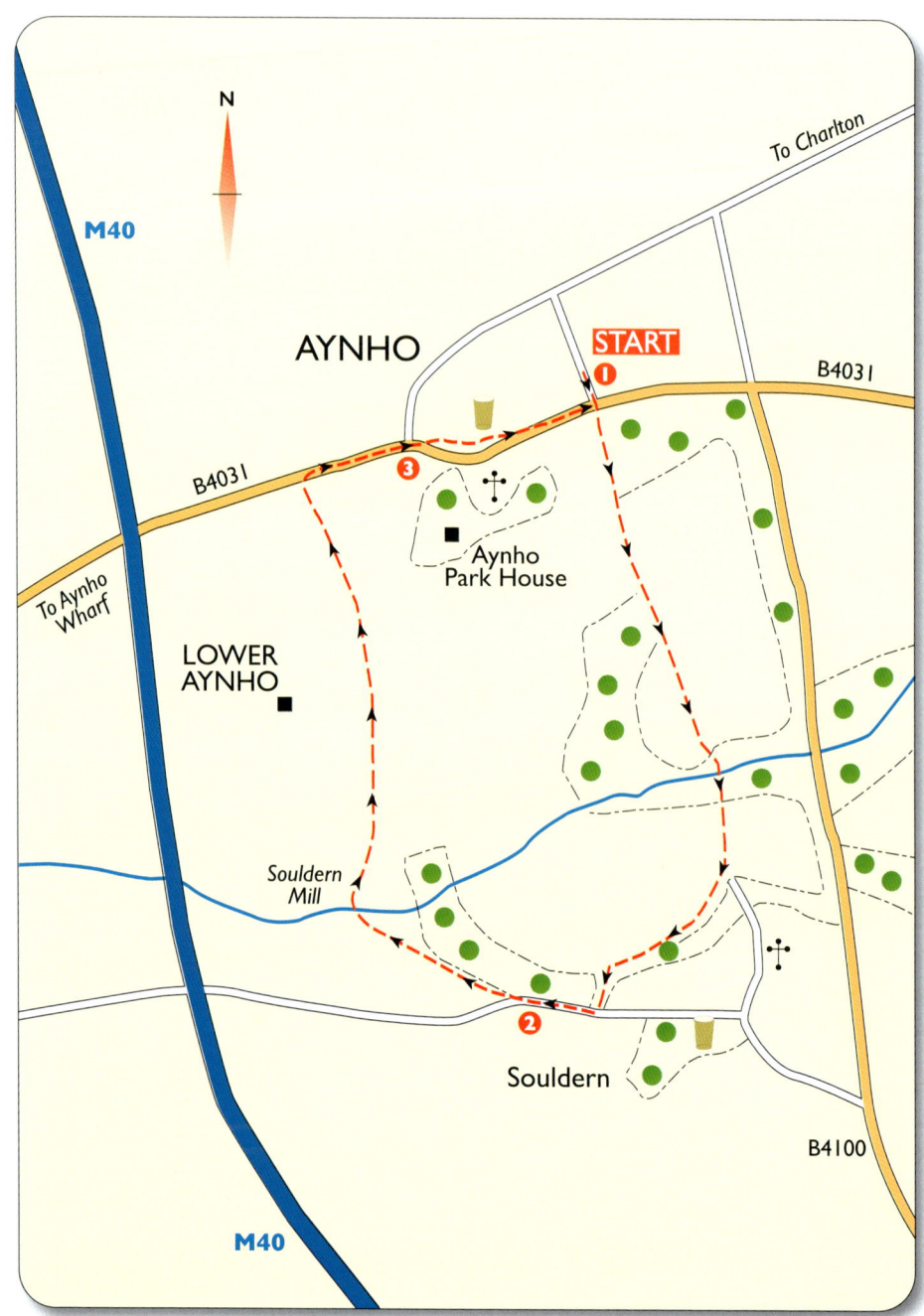

■ *Along the way* ■

fence at the end is a stone stile which you cross to join the road opposite the very imposing gates of **Souldern Manor**. Turn right here and walk along the road.

2 Where the road swings left, take the bridleway ahead signed to Aynho. Carry on along this path trying to keep a good pace for a mile, following the path around to the right at **Souldern Mill**. On reaching the road, turn right keeping the wall of **Aynho Park** on the right.

3 When the road junction is reached, cross over and go right then quickly left into **Little Lane**, a pretty route between houses and more of those drystone walls. If you would like to see the front of **Aynho House**, instead of turning up the lane carry on round the bend and rejoin the route by the **Cartwright Arms**. Carry on beside the road past the pub and notice those apricot trees on the cottage walls. Walk beside the main road back to the start.

9 Great Cransley

On the Level

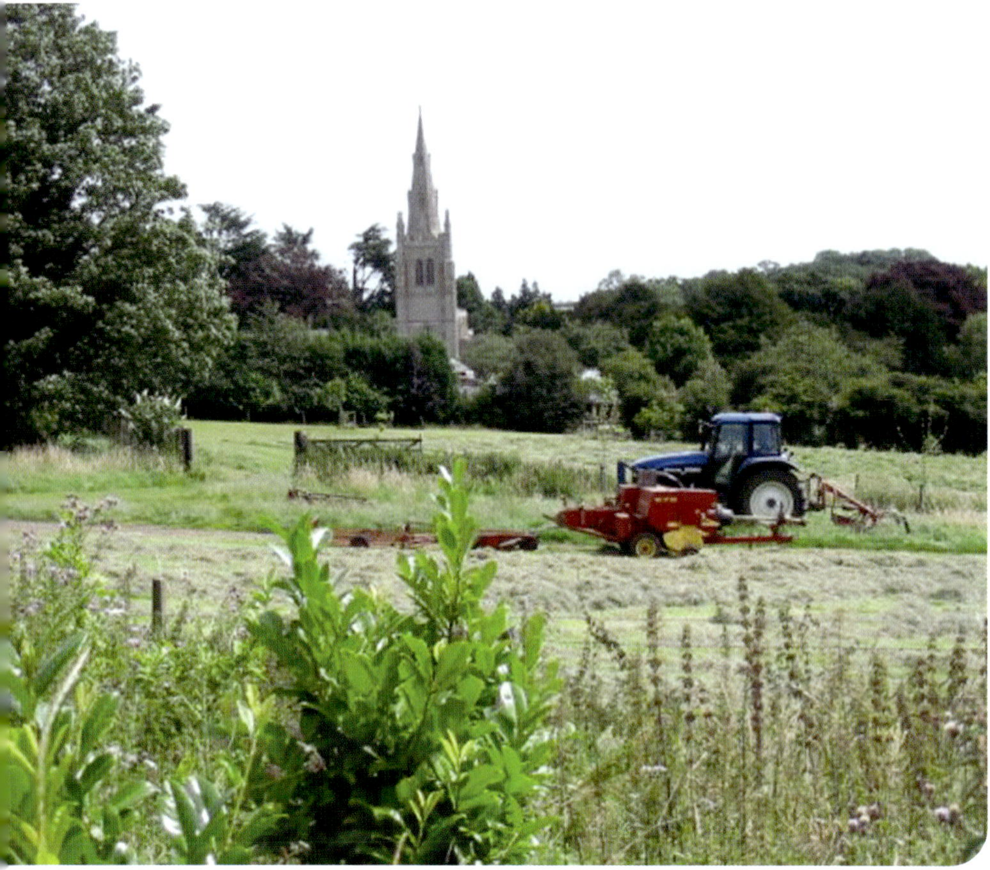

Great Cransley church seen from across the fields

Cransley Hall, passed on the route but not open to the public, was built in 1580 by Dame Alice Owen who, in 1613, founded the Dame Alice Owen School which still exists today in Potters Bar, Hertfordshire. Cransley also has a very pretty church which is worth a visit to see the stained-glass window with the three cranes which were part of the coat of arms of the family who lived in the manor and after whom the village was named. Cransley reservoir is not far away and heron are a

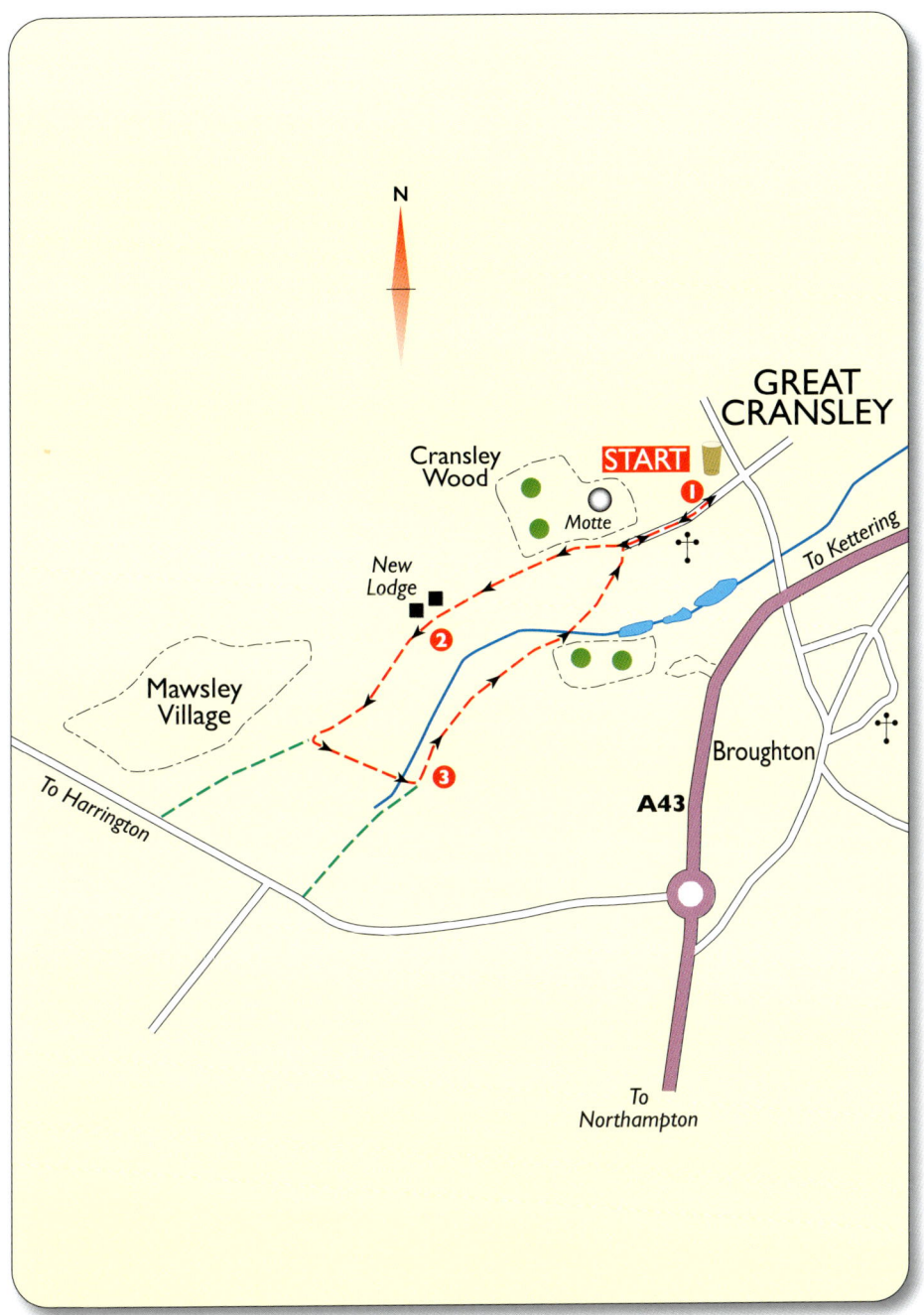

common sight there. Thanksgiving services were once held at the church for the American servicemen who were stationed in the area during the Second World War. They presented a stained-glass window showing Churchill and Roosevelt in conference over the Atlantic Charter.

From this small village starts a walk into the countryside with barely a slope in sight! This means, of course, that you can get up a good head of steam and you will do the 3 miles in record time.

1 Carry on along the lane with its overhanging trees passing **Cransley Hall** and the **church of St Andrew**. This lane is a delight, especially in spring when masses of snowdrops are in flower. Continue along the lane passing some pretty ironstone cottages until you come to the end. Carry on to the right along the bridleway, signed as a 'No through road for private vehicles'.

2 Now is the time to pick up speed. Continue along the bridleway with **Cransley Wood** on the right and open fields on the left. Bear round the wall of **New Lodge Farm** and join an obvious track going ahead under the overhead wires with two silos on the horizon. The new village of **Mawsley** can be seen to the right. Carry on to a T-junction where you turn left with the silos now on the right. At the next T-junction, turn left again.

GRADE: 2
ESTIMATED CALORIE BURN: 400

Distance: 3 miles
Time: 1¼ hours
Stiles: 0
Terrain: A level walk on farm roads, tracks and a couple of grassy fields.
Map: OS Explorer 224 Corby, Kettering & Wellingborough
Starting Point: The lane leading to the church in Great Cransley. GR 831768
How to get there: Great Cransley is 3 miles west of Kettering just off the A43. To get there you have to go into Broughton and take the turning off the main street signed to Great Cransley and Loddington. When approaching from this direction, take the first turning left into a lane marked as a bridleway and to the church.
Refreshments: The Three Cranes pub in Great Cransley serves lunch on Saturdays, Sundays and bank holidays. Telephone 01536 790287.

The route is well signed

3 Follow the track passing a line of trees. **Great Cransley church** can be seen peeping above the trees ahead, as well as the wonderful spire of Kettering parish church in the distance. Cross a track leading to a lone farm on the right and go through the metal gate into a field, usually full of sheep. Continue ahead down the slope to a wooden gate and then cross a little brick-sided bridge and keep beside the fence. If you think you deserve it having walked so fast, linger at this lovely spot for a rest and a drink. Keeping the fence on your right, go through a metal gate and carry on past a small cemetery on the left. Walk between the hawthorn hedges and rejoin the road. Turn right, back to your start.

■ *'A leisurely lunch in the sun'* ■

10 *Charlton*

In the Cherwell Valley

FOOTPATHS
FOR FITNESS

■ *On the way to Walton Grounds* ■

Charlton is a pretty village that sits near the centre of a triangle of towns including Aynho, Banbury and Brackley. One would never think that a few miles west lies the Cherwell valley, containing the busy M40, the Oxford Canal, the River Cherwell and the railway line. Such surprises are to be found throughout this charming county which are only chanced upon by those who use their own two feet.

> **GRADE: 2**
> **ESTIMATED CALORIE BURN: 500**
>
> **Distance:** 3½ miles
> **Time:** 1½ hours
> **Stiles:** 1
> **Terrain:** One long slope, and a hill back into Charlton, otherwise on level field paths and tracks.
> **Map:** OS Explorer 191 Banbury, Bicester & Chipping Norton
> **Starting point:** Beside the road near the Rose and Crown. GR 528358.
> **How to get there:** Turn off west from the A43 south of Brackley signed to Charlton and Kings Sutton. In Charlton, turn left onto the Aynho road and park near the Rose & Crown.
> **Refreshments:** The Rose & Crown in Charlton. Telephone 01295 811317.

This delightful walk takes you out into the fields towards Kings Sutton, with panoramic views of the Cherwell valley, returning via a hill fort.

1 With the **Rose & Crown** on your right, walk down the road. Ignore a footpath sign to **Kings Sutton** and turn right onto a tarmac track opposite **Garage Cottage**. Continue down and through a metal gate into the field where you go diagonally right to a waymarker on a wooden gate leading to a stile and crossing a footbridge over a stream. Turn left with the brook and hedge beside you, then over another footbridge before carrying on ahead.

The next waymarker is on what seems to be a somewhat superfluous footbridge so continue along beside the noise of rushing water (a suggestion perhaps that you too might up the pace a bit!). The next footbridge on the left is definitely needed so that you can cross the stream and turn right with the brook and trees now on your right. Go through the wide gap in the hedge and straight on across the middle of the next field. The farmer has left an obvious track through the field ahead. You then join a wide track on the left and have the opportunity to stride out. Ahead of you over on the right are some barns at **Walton Grounds**. Carry on to the end of the track where it meets a bridleway leading over the hill to **Aynho**. You will see a waymarker on the left which you follow going left.

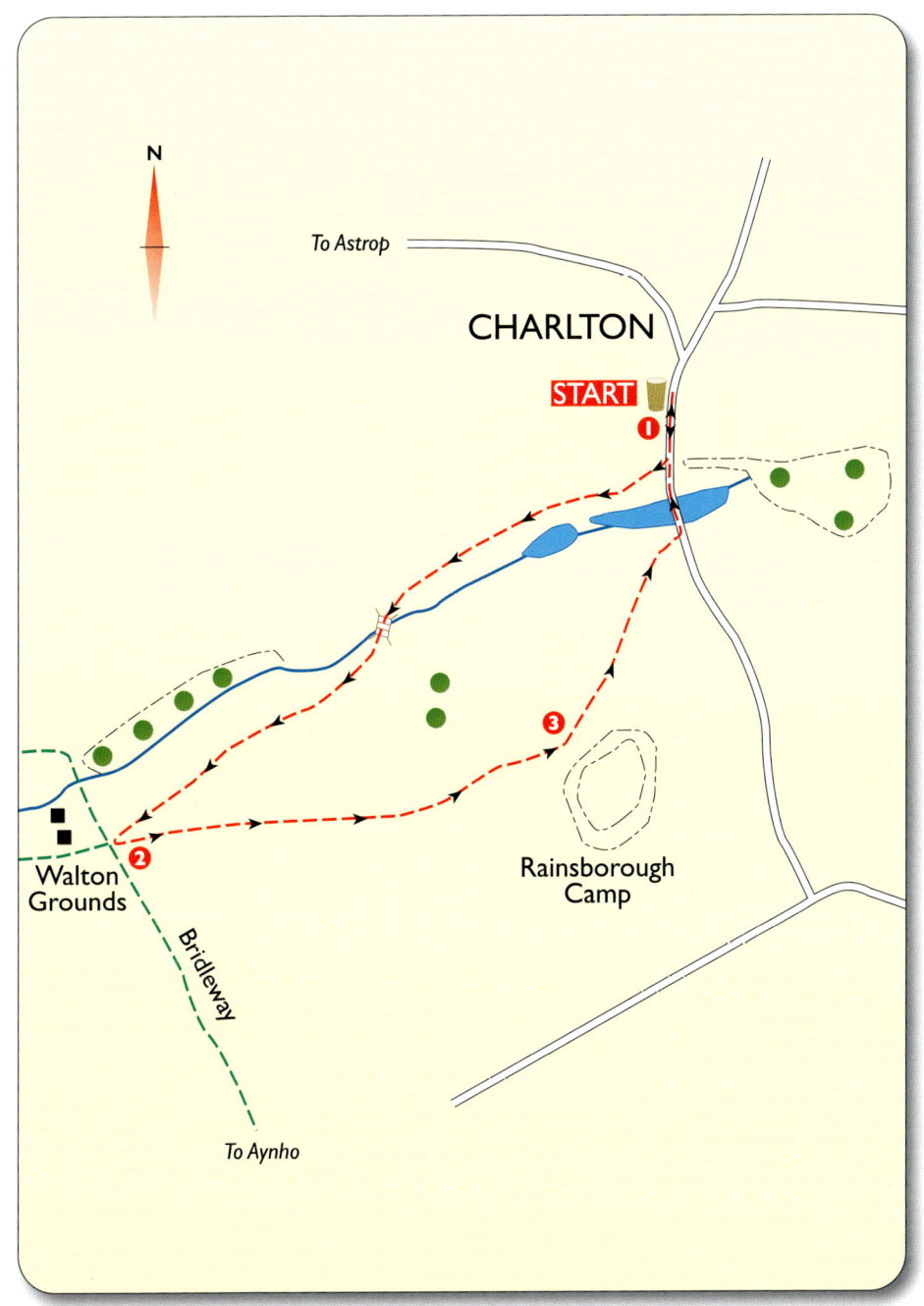

■ Panoramic views await you ■

2 Once again the farmer has left a path going slightly right and up to the top of the rise towards the trees. This is quite a long slow pull but as ever, the reward is at the top when you turn round to admire the panoramic view of the Cherwell valley. Go through the gap in the trees and follow the bridleway marker keeping the hedge on your right. Over to the left ahead you will see the village of **Charlton**. Some 50 yards short of the end of the field turn right through the gate and go left beside the hedge. Just over to the right a mound can be seen which is an Iron Age fort called **Rainsborough Camp**, a scheduled monument. Constructed in the 4th/5th century BC and covering an area of about six acres, it burnt down in 150 BC and the site was then unoccupied until the Romans arrived in AD 250.

3 Continue through the wooden gates having read the history of the fort, and go through a metal gate with a white disc. The waymarking is not good here so cross the field in a straight line towards a very large oak tree in the hedge opposite and a wooden farm gate. Go through the gate and then bear right to the end of the fence opposite a waymarker. Carry on beside the trees with a wooden fence on the left until you arrive at the road where you turn left, cross the babbling brook and finish with an uphill flourish.

■ *The masterly art of drystone walling* ■

In the Land of the Potters

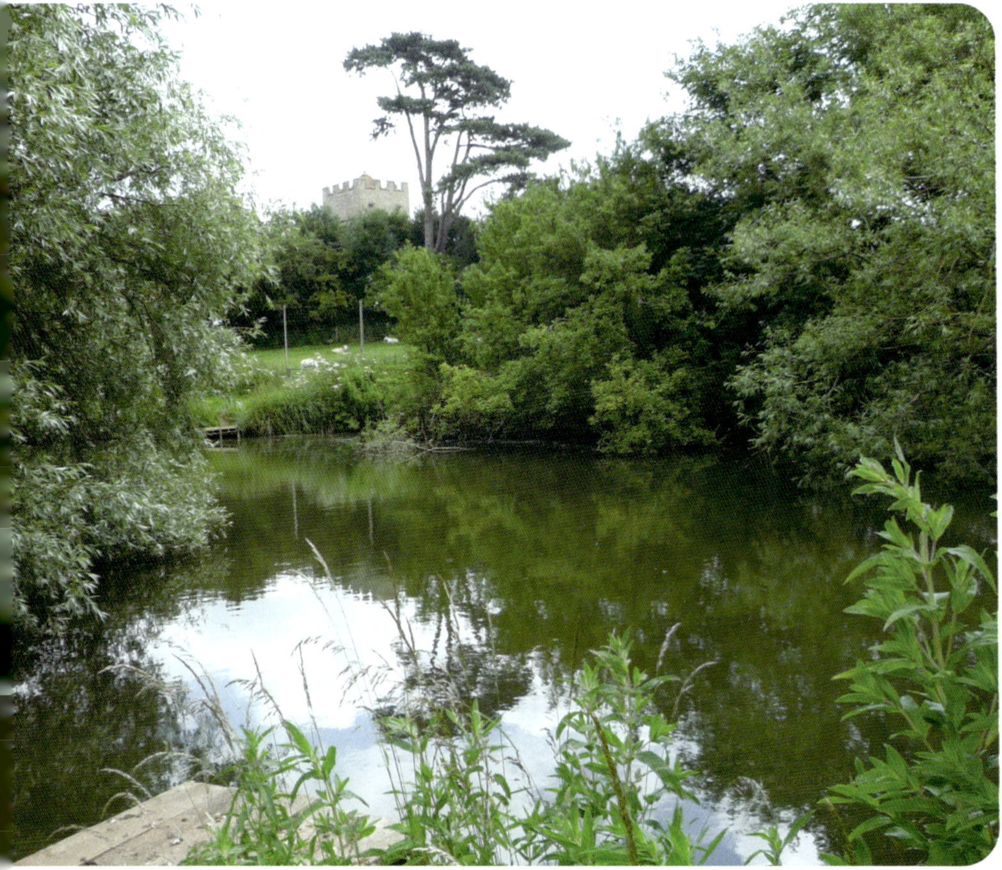

■ *The duck pond at point 3 of the route* ■

The interesting village of Potterspury lies on Watling Street, the old Roman road. Its name is derived from the 12th-century pottery kilns that used to be here. The church of St Nicholas, built in 1087, is the starting point from where you will go out through fields to Yardley Gobion, walk a short length of a canal towpath and return through attractive countryside on a section of the Grafton Way, a 13-mile, long-distance path following the Grand Union Canal from Milton Keynes to Greens Norton.

1 Turn left from the church onto **Yardley Road** passing the **United Reformed Church**. Continue up to a large bend in the road where you will see a footpath sign. Take the path going straight ahead into a large field signed **Grafton Way**. The path veers right out of the second field, at which point turn right towards some houses keeping the hedge on your right. Ignore the waymarker and swing left with the hedge now on the left and houses on the right. Carry on again through the next field, go through the kissing gate and obliquely right. Follow the waymarker and the post saying 'Grafton Way' leading towards a brick building which is the **Yardley Gobion recreation centre**. Go through the kissing gate, then right onto **School Lane**. Meet the main road and turn left. Go right at the T-junction towards the **Meadows Care Home** and past some pretty thatched cottages. Turn left at a grassy triangle signed to **Grafton Regis** and **Stoney Stratford**. Carry on down to the main A508 and cross over going towards a large wooden barn.

2 Walk down the road leading to **Old Wharf Farm** and, just before a sign saying 'No entry except on business', you will see a metal gate to the right of a mirror and a signpost directing you onto a public bridleway. Cross the field going left towards a fenced-off area, usually with horses in it. Go through the gate and carry on ahead towards an obvious gap in the hedge where you pass through two gates. Turn left and cross the white painted bridge over the **Grand Union Canal** and immediately right, down to the

GRADE: 2
ESTIMATED CALORIE BURN: 600

Distance: 3½ miles
Time: 2 hours
Stiles: 3
Terrain: Mainly level on roads and field paths.
Map: OS Explorer 207 Newport Pagnell & Northampton South
Starting point: St Nicholas church, Potterspury. GR 763433
How to get there: Potterspury is on the A5, 5 miles south of Towcester and just north of Milton Keynes. Travelling north from Milton Keynes, take the first turning to Potterspury and carry on down into the village passing the Cock pub on the left. The church can be seen set back from a green where there is plenty of parking.
Refreshments: The Cock Inn, Potterspury. Telephone: 01908 542142.

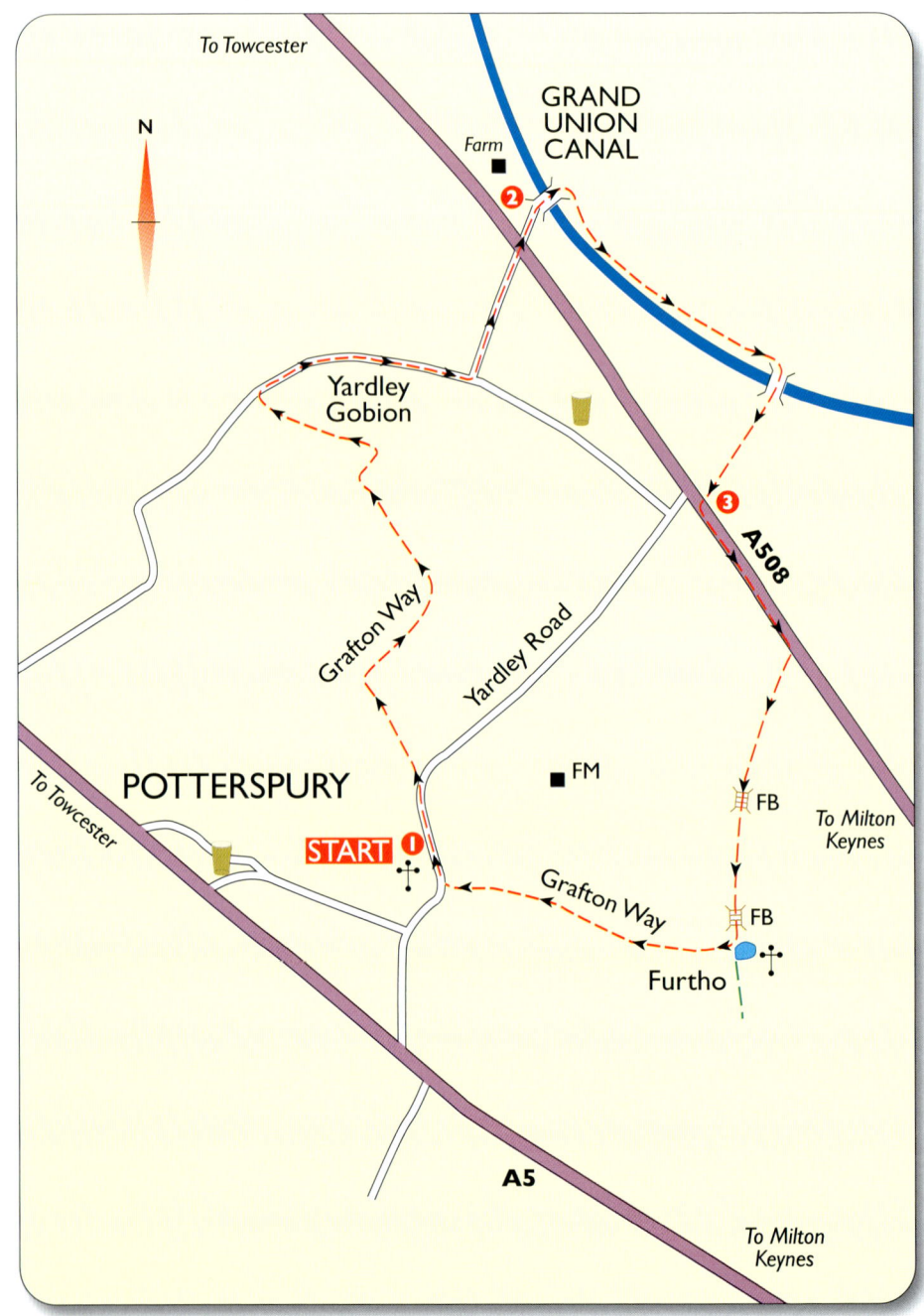

■ *A shady spot* ■

towpath. Walk along past one bridge and, on reaching the second bridge, go up to the left and cross over the canal onto a track going uphill. Keep left with the hedge on your right. Climb the stile and, with due care, cross the road going left.

3 Walk along the pavement past the sign advertising free-range eggs at Manor farm, until a very obvious track appears on the right with a bridleway sign. Go through the gap in the hedge and take the line of the waymarker. The path is rather uneven here, with the odd burrow entrance concealed by the lush undergrowth. Continue along this track, crossing three wooden footbridges, after which turn right and climb the stile into an idyllic area with a duck pond and a view of **Furtho church** across it. Continue round the pond, in the direction of a wooden barn, but very soon head for the hedge on the right and go through the kissing gate into the field, then through two kissing gates onto the **Grafton Way**. Follow the direction of the waymarker heading for a large white disc beside a kissing gate. Take good care here, the plank crossing the ditch immediately after the gate is narrow. Continue following the waymarkers noticing **St Nicholas's church** ahead. Finally climb a stile and continue back to the church.

12 Hellidon

The Heights of Hellidon

■ *The clear path through the fields* ■

This truly rural walk explores some of the lovely undulating countryside in the area. Arbury Hill, the highest point in the county at 738 ft, is to the east of Hellidon which sits at the foot of Windmill Hill. Stone buildings gather round the church where, after the Second World War, a beehive was found in the belfry and a hundredweight of honey kept the population going for nigh on a year! This walk follows the contours with a few gentle hills that might have you puffing a little but that's all to the good!

1 Leave the little green down **Catesby End** following the sign to the gated road to **Catesby**. Go through the kissing gate onto the **Jurassic Way** and walk ahead for approximately ½ mile ignoring footpath signs until the road zigzags. Take the path off right through a kissing gate down towards a small, red-brick barn and thence to a large oak tree with a waymarker directing you left to a wooden gate in a fence. Over on the right is **Catesby House**. Follow the line of the waymarker which goes towards the house and climb the stile onto a track.

2 Turn right and head for a footpath sign going off to the right. Walk uphill aiming for the top left of the field between some barns and trees. Pause awhile to recover your breath and turn round to admire the wonderful panorama before climbing the stile. Turn left. If you are particularly tall and athletic, climb the stile; if not, go through the gate. Carry on ahead, watching your footing – the odd tree root can catch you unawares. The bridleway sign leads up to the farmyard but the footpath actually goes diagonally right across the field to a gate in the corner to join the farm road. As you walk along here the 3,000-yard **Catesby Tunnel** is beneath your feet. This was part of the Great Central Railway opened in 1897 as an extension from Marylebone to Nottingham Victoria. The story is that it went underground because the then owners of Catesby House objected to an overground line. The tunnel was closed in 1966. Carry on ahead to the road.

3 Cross the road and follow the direction of the waymarker. On reaching the red-brick house by a slight bend in the path, there is a wooden footbridge

GRADE: 2
ESTIMATED CALORIE BURN: 700

Distance: 3¾ miles
Time: 2 hours
Stiles: 6
Terrain: Mostly on field paths and tracks
Map: OS Explorer 206 Edge Hill & Fenny Compton
Starting point: The small green at Catesby End. GR 515584
How to get there: Hellidon is well signed off the A361 Daventry–Banbury road just north of Charwelton. Turn left in front of the Red Lion and follow the road round and downhill until you reach a small green with a stone pillar box. Park in the environs.
Refreshments: The Red Lion at Hellidon. Telephone: 01327 261200.

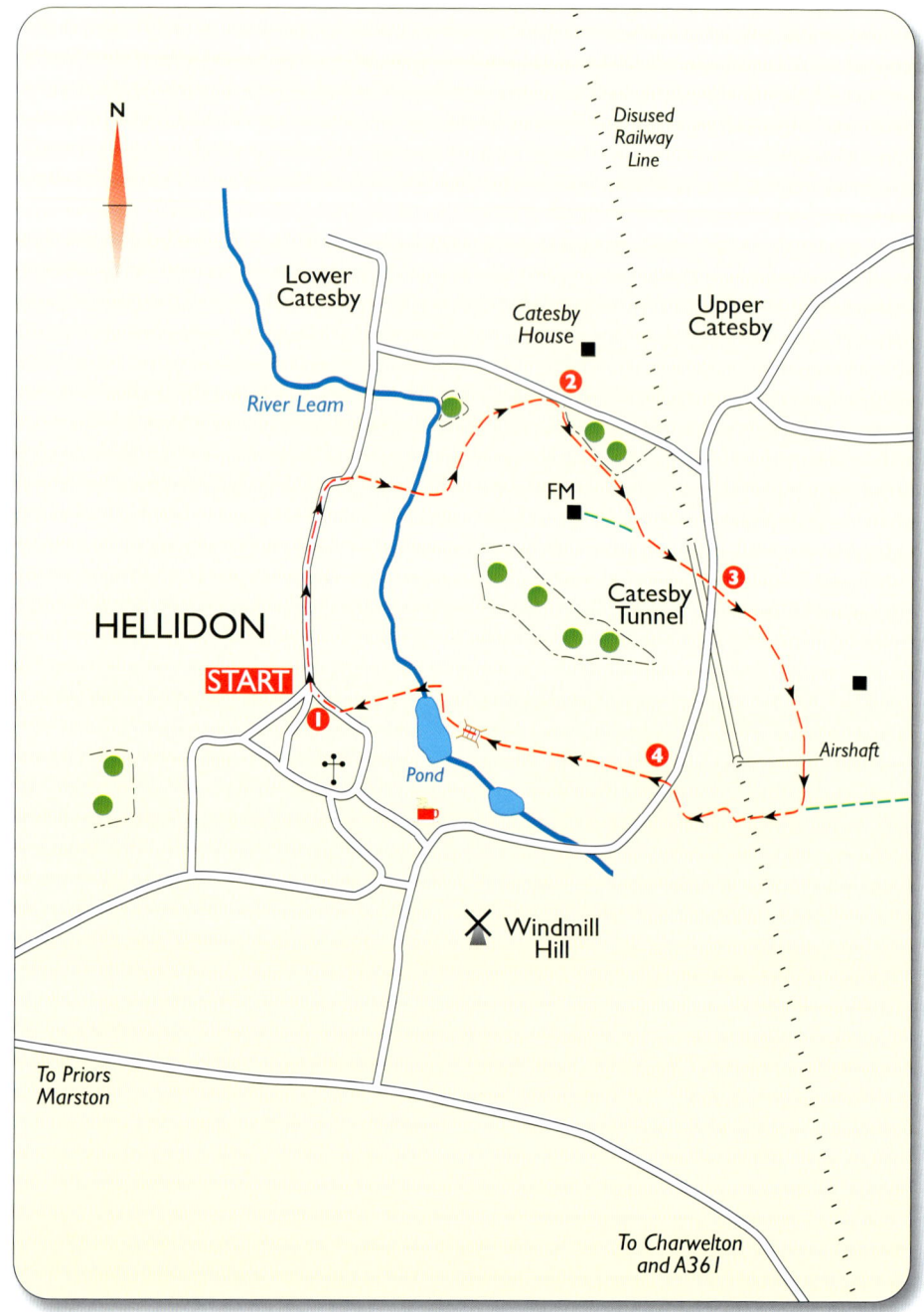

N

Disused
Railway
Line

Lower
Catesby

River Leam

Catesby
House

Upper
Catesby

2

FM

HELLIDON

Catesby
Tunnel

3

START

1

Pond

4

Airshaft

Windmill
Hill

To Priors
Marston

To Charwelton
and A361

■ *Friendly locals!* ■

well hidden in the hedge on the right. Cross it, climb the stile and enter the field. The waymarker would have you visiting the house so instead make for the left-hand end of the fence opposite. Cross the track and walk through the metal gate into a large field which may be full of cattle. Carry on to the bottom right where you leave the field by way of a wooden gate. Glance to the right to see one of the air shafts of the tunnel. Continue ahead on the bridleway round a little pond. Turn left after going through a metal gate and down to a track which you cross. Follow the waymarker which leads through a private garden and join the road.

4 Turn right and walk along the grass verge for 100 yards or so and then cross over to a bridleway sign. Here is another uphill path to test your fitness but, as always, you are rewarded with a lovely view for your efforts. Over to the left are the remains of a windmill on **Windmill Hill** and beautiful views of

the soft Northamptonshire countryside. Carry on through two gates to the bottom and keep the hedge on the right as you near a tranquil pond with ducks and trees reflected in the water. Just before the pond, cross the wooden footbridge on the right and follow the direction of the arrow having gone up a slight slope into the field. Soon on the left is a handrail beside some rather hidden steps leading down to the other end of the pond via a kissing gate. Continue over the slope bearing right towards a house. Just before a small pond go over two stiles on the right. Turn left and go through two metal gates to return to the road and the green.

■ *A tranquil oasis* ■

13 Flore

A Hidden Gem

FOOTPATHS FOR FITNESS

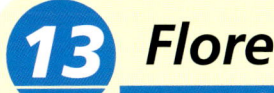

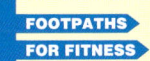

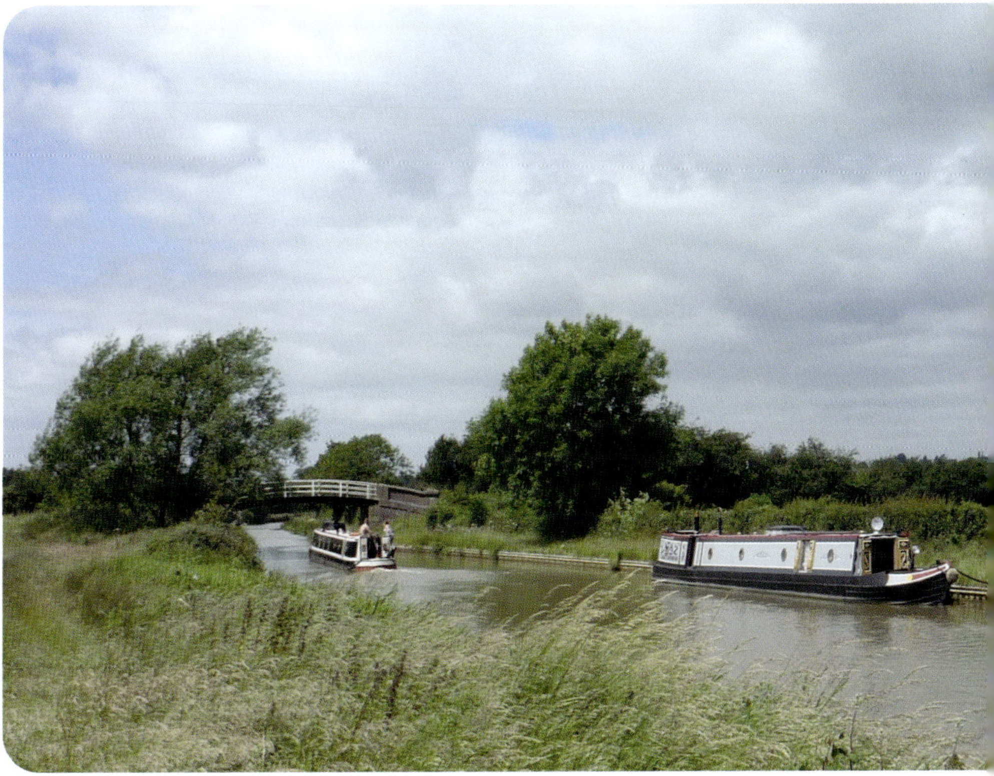

■ *The Grand Union Canal* ■

Like many of our beautiful Northamptonshire villages, it is easy to drive through Flore without realising what gems lie hidden off the main road. The walk starts in the tranquil churchyard of All Saints where Quakers, John and Sarah Adams are buried. They are thought to have been the parents of John Adams, second President of the United States of America and the grandparents of John Quincey Adams, the sixth president. The church itself has remarkable medieval doors.

This is a fairly flat route giving you the opportunity to walk briskly and get the heart pumping. It goes out into the fields, along the Grand Union Canal towpath and returns to Flore through the fields via Nether Heyford.

1 Cross the church car park and enter the tranquil churchyard with its lovely mature trees and pretty ironstone church. Cross in the direction of the **Nene Way** footpath sign leaving through a kissing gate into a field. The signs continue to give good directions to the road where you will see the back of a white-painted building.

2 Cross the busy road with care and proceed ahead up a wide stony track. The gradient is only slight so there is a chance here to speed up a bit. Immediately before the bridge, take the flight of wooden steps down to the **Grand Union Canal** and turn left along the towpath picking up speed as you enjoy looking at the busy canal traffic and the array of boats at the marina. Go under the A5 and shortly you will see a sign telling you that Braunston is but ten miles away so when your level of fitness increases, there's another walk to tackle! When you arrive at the next bridge, leave the canal and go up to the road. Turn left going downhill and shortly after the bend and opposite a large dead tree a footpath sign points over a stile into a field.

3 From this point the markers are very good, leading you from field to field over stiles and footbridges and under power lines. (Be aware that the little wooden footbridge after the duck pond which you will see on the right has some raised metal studs at either end on which one could easily trip.)

GRADE: 2
ESTIMATED CALORIE BURN: 800

Distance: 4½ miles
Time: 2 hours
Stiles: 4
Terrain: Easy level walking through fields and along a canal towpath.
Map: OS Explorer 223 Northampton & Market Harborough
Starting point: All Saints church in Flore. GR 642599
How to get there: Flore is approximately 1½ miles west of junction 16 of the M1 and 5 miles east of Daventry on the A45. All Saints church is signed off the main road towards the western end of the village.
Refreshments: The Paddocks Tearoom (telephone: 01327 340918) attached to the nursery and farm shop in Bliss Lane which is signed off the main road through Flore. There are also two pubs in Flore: the Royal Oak and the White Hart.

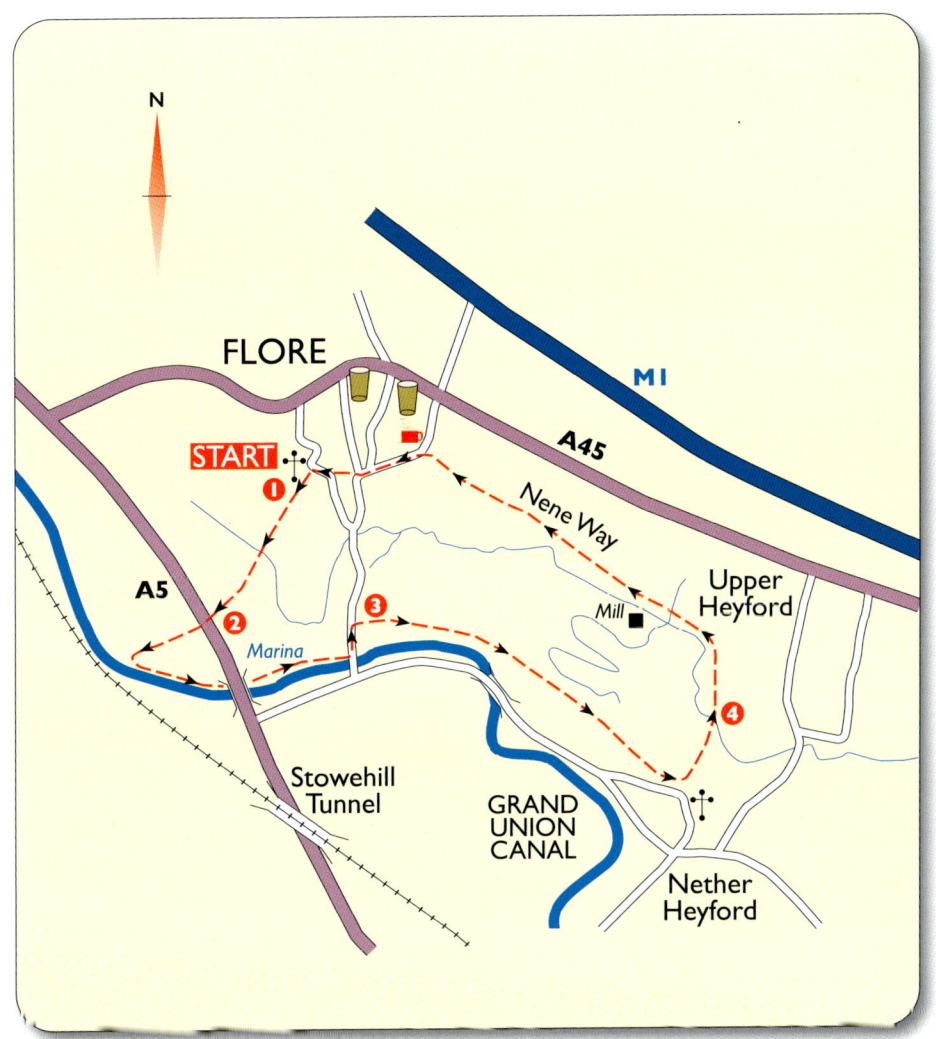

The church of **Nether Heyford** can be seen ahead. On meeting a stone track, turn right and, after about 30 yards, turn left over the low, rather hidden, stile into a field. Continue ahead, eventually meeting a long brick wall but just short of it turn left and follow the hedge to a gap behind some houses. Go through and turn left down the narrow track beside a brook, turning left over a bridge at the end and through a kissing gate onto the grassy track once used to bring flour to the village from the mill a little further on.

■ *All Saints church at Flore* ■

4 The **Nene Way** is well signed from here. Go past the mill and cross the wooden footbridge. Carry on straight ahead with wooden fencing on your left. Cross another footbridge, keep to the right of the pylon, heading in the direction of a large house. Continue walking through the fields and kissing gates. In the last field, you could turn sharp right to a well-signed tearoom, farm shop and nursery. This is the **Paddocks tearoom** as mentioned in the Refreshments section and is within ½ mile or so of the end of the walk. If you decide against the temptation, then walk towards a bungalow and leave the field to the right of it through a kissing gate beside a farm gate going between unusual thatched cob walls. Continue in the direction of the **Nene Way** sign and where a road comes in from the right further along, turn up this road and then left along **Spring Lane** which runs behind houses. Go through the barrier and return to the church.

14 Ravensthorpe

A Wildlife Wonderland

FOOTPATHS FOR FITNESS

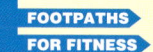

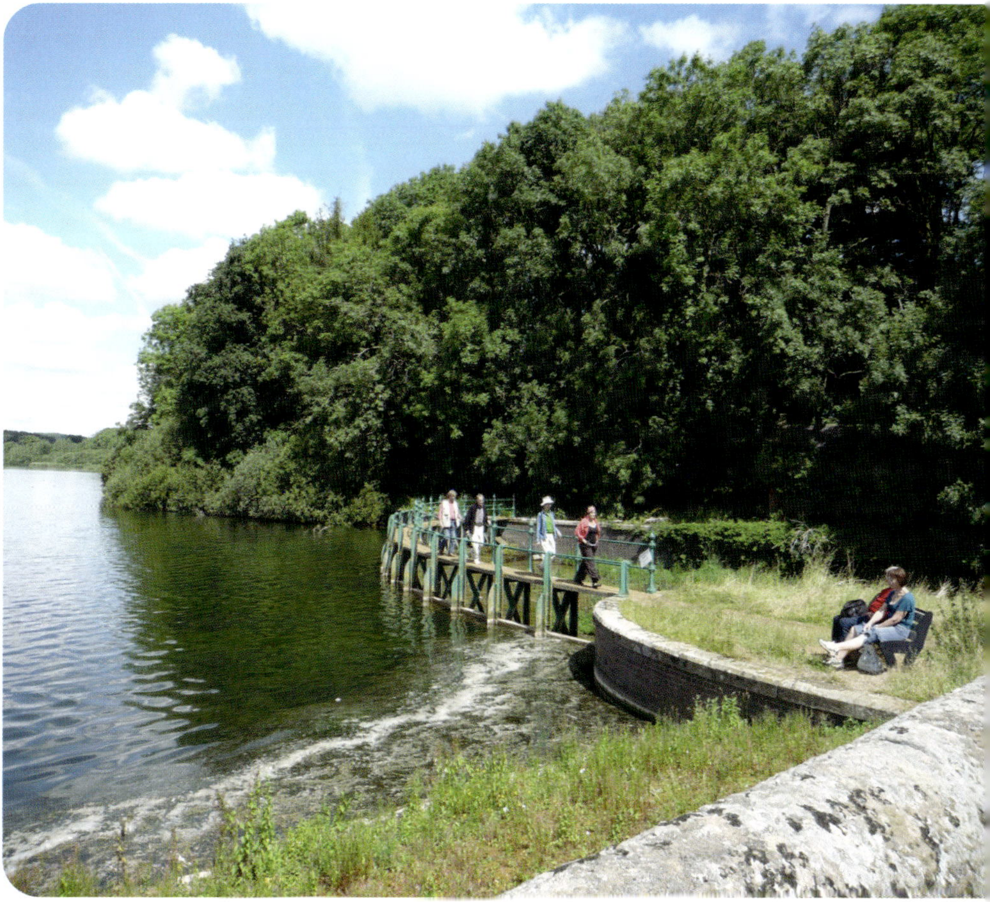

■ *The reservoir is a popular place for walkers* ■

Ravensthorpe Water is one of the most important wildlife sanctuaries in Europe. Your walk around it will be a real treat though fishermen and serious birdwatchers need permits here and you will need to be aware of backcasting by the anglers. This reservoir and nearby Hollowell reservoir were constructed in Victorian times to supply water to Northampton.

The route goes through wooded areas near the water's edge on one side and then across the dam giving open views of the reservoir. The route continues near the water's edge and then a short walk along the causeway to the car park. In the village of Coton, ¼ mile to the north, is Coton Manor whose truly delightful gardens and café are open to the public from the end of March to the end of September. Telephone: 01604 740219.

1 Having parked in the car park among various wildfowl, climb the very low stile beside the gate and proceed along a wide track which is densely wooded on the right and rather more open on the left. From time to time the sparkling waters of the reservoir can be glimpsed through the trees. Continue for some distance along the path enjoying the wildlife until, just short of a small brick building, an obvious track leads right down towards the water.

2 Cross the catwalk going across the reservoir to the dam and turn right on reaching it. You can now step out along this track at a good pace admiring the tranquil scene with the anglers' boats reflected in the water.

3 On reaching the little fishing lodge, pass behind it (there are public toilets here) and carry on along the path which can be boggy at times. Dragonflies

GRADE: 2
ESTIMATED CALORIE BURN: 700

Distance: 3 miles
Time: 1 hour
Stiles: 2
Terrain: The walk is all on the level and mostly on firm ground but boots are a necessity as it can be muddy.
Map: OS Explorer 223 Northampton & Market Harborough
Starting point: The car park beside the reservoir. GR 677712
How to get there: From Ravensthorpe, take the road signed to Coton and Guilsborough and then the small road signed off to the right to Hollowell and Creaton. Just as the road bends left you will see an Anglian Water sign on the right at the entrance to the car park.
Refreshments: The Ward Arms at Guilsborough. Telephone: 01604 740265.

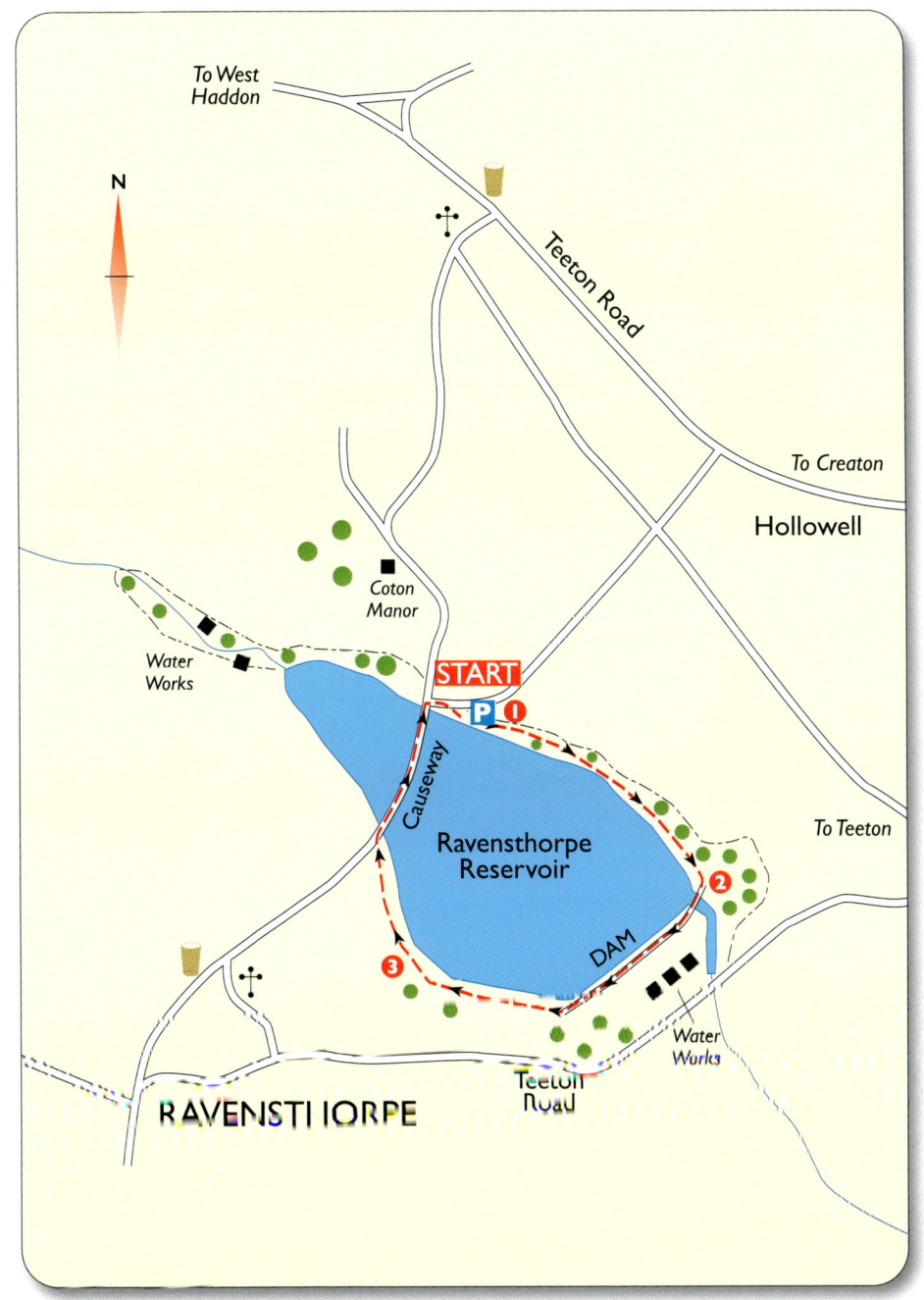

N

To West
Haddon

Teeton Road

To Creaton

Hollowell

Coton
Manor

Water
Works

START

P

Causeway

Ravensthorpe
Reservoir

To Teeton

DAM

Water
Works

RAVENSTHORPE

Teeton
Road

■ *Hoping for a catch* ■

abound in this area. Climb the stile which leads to the road between Ravensthorpe and Coton and turn right to return to the start.

15 Great Addington
Water, Water, Everywhere

■ *A colourful springtime garden in Woodford* ■

Great Addington and the surrounding villages are steeped in history. The route of a Roman road leads from here up to 'Twelve Church View' on the Woodford road near which, on the highest point, are three tumuli dating back over a thousand years. At Shooters Hill, between Little Addington and Great Addington, an Anglo-Saxon burial ground was found and a burial urn unearthed nearby now resides in the British Museum, putting Addington firmly on the map.

This is an ideal spot from which to set off on many different walks. Our route takes you across beautiful water meadows, over millstreams and beside lakes created by gravel extraction. Wildlife abounds. The Nene Way, which eventually goes to the Wash, passes through the area. This 70-mile long-distance path stretches from Badby, near Daventry, to Wansford. It follows a particularly scenic route through pretty villages and towns.

GRADE: 2
ESTIMATED CALORIE BURN: 800

Distance: 4½ miles
Time: 2 hours
Stiles: 3
Terrain: Mostly on the level with just a bit of a puff at times in the last half mile.
Map: OS Explorer 224 Corby, Kettering & Wellingborough
Starting point: The village hall car park opposite the church unless there is a function, in which case, beside the road. GR 958751
How to get there: From junction 11 of the A14 follow the signs to Great Addington or turn off the A6 at Irthlingborough and follow signs north to the village.
Refreshments: The Hare and Hounds in Great Addington serves lunches every day. The pub also has a small shop attached to it. Telephone: 01536 330521.

1 Walk straight down **Main Street** with the **Hare and Hounds** on the left and the Manor entrance on the right. Go down **Lower Street** and immediately before an electricity substation, turn left over the stile and follow the footpath beside the brook. Cross the footbridge and turn right with the brook and then bear left towards the waymarker beside the hedge. Carry on straight ahead keeping the hedge on the left going towards the lake.

2 Turn right and follow the lake round to an obvious footbridge which you cross. Keeping beside the old stepping stones, head for another footbridge on a mound. Cross this and keep on the track past a lock gate and over a little bridge. Water lilies and irises abound in season and the cuckoo makes its presence felt. Pass a yellow barrier and a few yards further on turn left through a wooden gate. This is the start of a stretch of disused railway line which heads for **Thrapston**. The opposite way leads to **Stanwick Lakes** recreational centre where there are cycle paths, picnic areas, adventure trails and much more. Now here is the chance to put your new-found fitness to the test.

3 This is a path full of interest with lots of newly-planted trees of every variety. It is shared with cyclists and horses. On the right you will see anglers on the trout fishery and boats at the **Willy Watt Mill**. Shortly after going under the

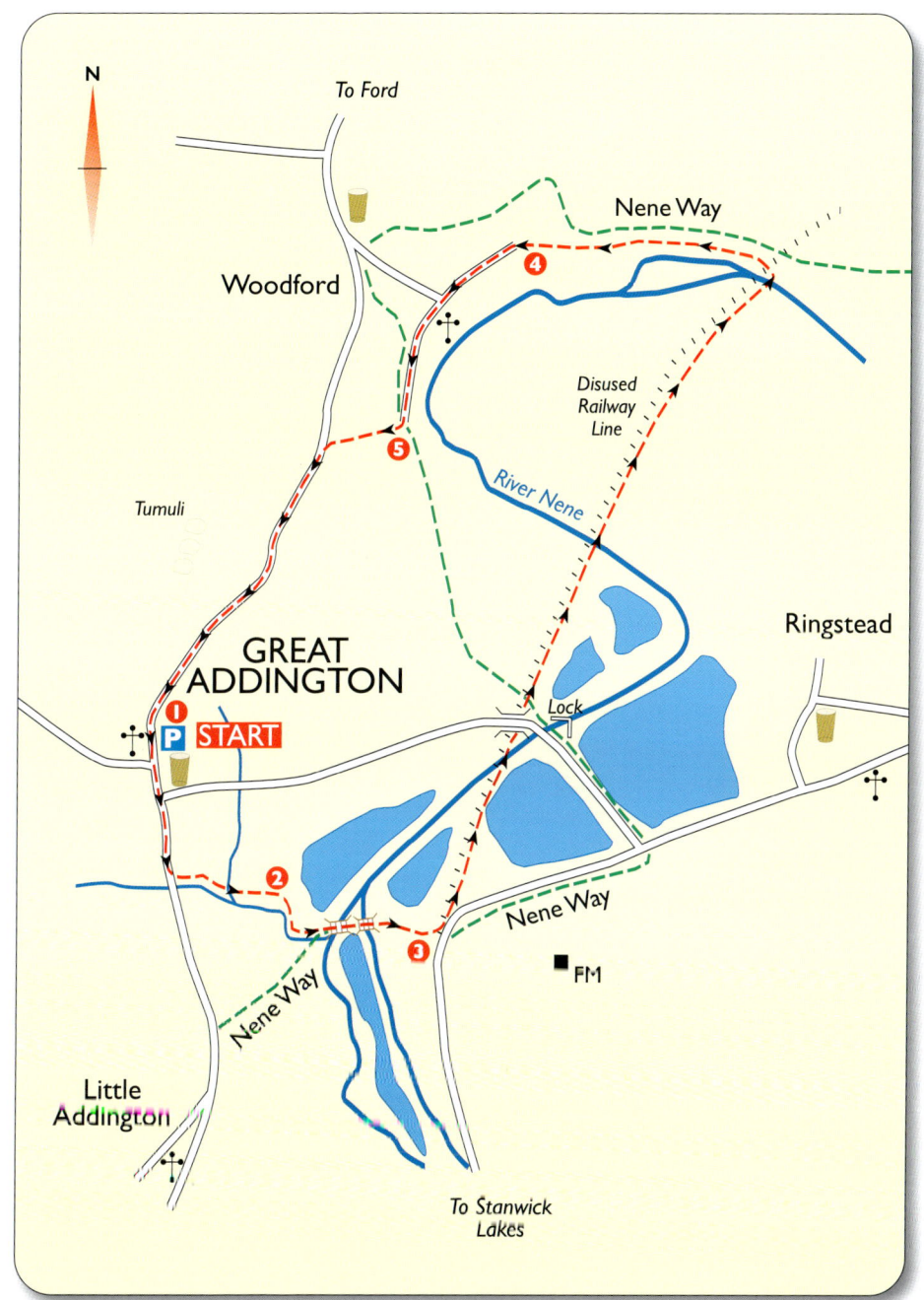

N

To Ford

Woodford

Nene Way

Disused
Railway
Line

River Nene

Tumuli

**GREAT
ADDINGTON**

Ringstead

P **START**

Lock

Nene Way

Nene Way

FM

Little
Addington

To Stanwick
Lakes

■ *The watermeadows* ■

first road bridge there is a **Nene Way** sign pointing left. Carry on along this track for 1½ miles at a good pace if you can. Various bridges both underfoot and overhead will be passed and when you come to the last bridge for you, you will notice a widening in the river where once there was a mill but now there is a lock gate. On the right is a wonderfully picturesque line of trees reflected in the river. A few yards on from the bridge is a waymarker signing left onto a path beside the river.

4 Follow the path and where you come to some wire fencing take the left fork heading for a metal gate and the road. Go straight along past the church to the end of the road and over the stile into a field. Bear right up the slope to a metal gate and stile. Cross the field heading for a metal gate in the top left corner.

5 Continue up the concrete road and turn left into the road ahead. It is a bit of a pull up here but it doesn't last long and you will be rewarded with a rest at the top when you can pause and see if you can spot the twelve churches visible on a clear day! To the right there are three Bronze Age burial mounds pillaged long ago. Downhill now for a bit and then up into Great Addington and a well earned low calorie drink!

■ *The old railway line from Northampton to Peterborough* ■
along the Nene Valley

16 Harrington

Ups and Downs

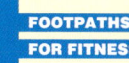

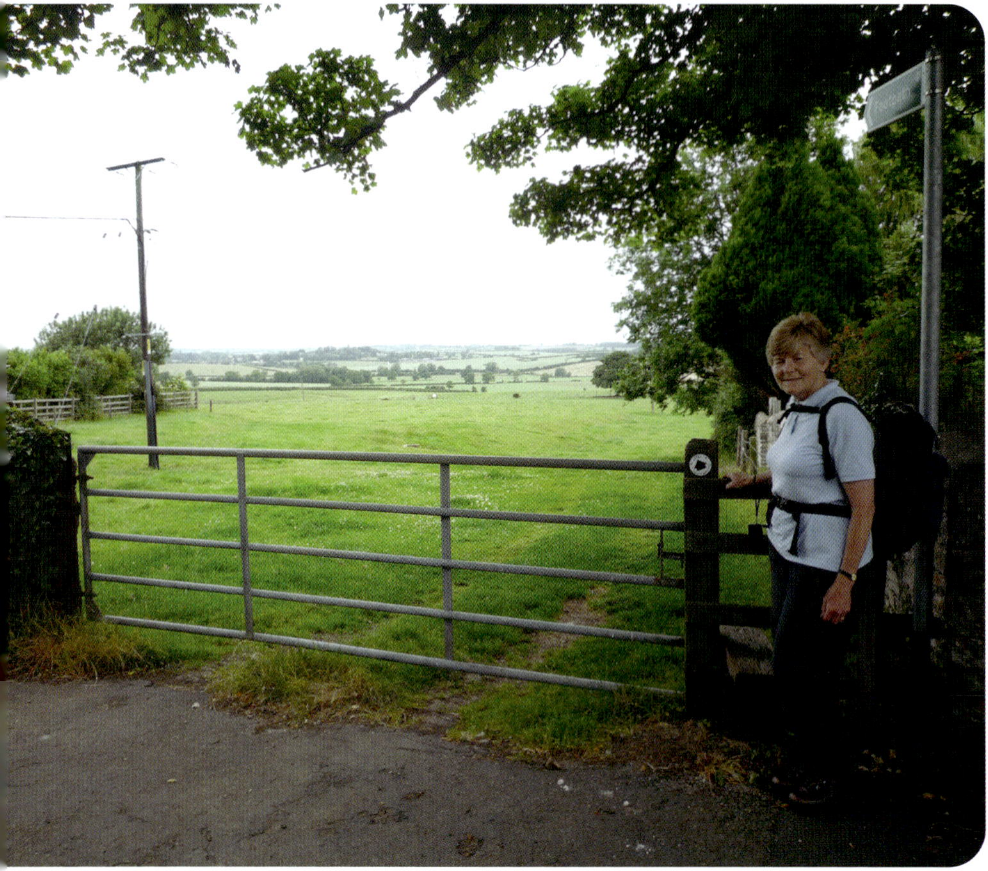

■ *All kitted up and ready to go!* ■

This small village has had quite a history one way and another. After the Dissolution of the Monasteries in the 16th century, the manor passed through the hands of several families, the last being the Tollemaches after whom the local pub is named. The manor was pulled down in 1745 and the remains of terraces and fishponds that once supplied the monastic house can still be seen. In 1883 an attempt was made to bore for coal but the area was found to be the sight of an extinct volcano!

The walk is very varied and full of interest as you walk through wooded areas and fields. An excellent information board fills in the details of the terrain.

1 From the **Tollemache Arms**, turn right along the village street passing a long row of stone cottages and keeping a stone wall on the right (over which a good view opens up) until you pass the village hall and then turn right at the bridleway sign. Go through a large metal gate and follow the direction of the waymarker. On the left is an information board with interesting facts about this area and an explanation for all the humps and hollows. Continue downhill and then up a wide grassy track with hedges on either side. **Warren Hill Farm** can be seen over to the left. Where the track swings left, continue with it along the bottom of the field with the hedge on the right and then uphill towards the farm. You will doubtless feel that your heart has been well exercised, so turn around and admire the view across the landscape. At the bottom of this track go through a metal farm gate into a grassy field, usually dotted with sheep, and head for the farm gate. Cross the attractive little bridge beside a ford.

2 At this point, you can make a short detour and go diagonally left uphill to a gate and the road leading left to visit the village of **Arthingworth**. To continue the walk, though, turn right here following the barbed-wire fence to a gate with a waymarker. Continue to follow the markers uphill towards

GRADE: 2
ESTIMATED CALORIE BURN: 700

Distance: 5 miles
Time: 2 hours
Stiles: 1
Terrain: Mainly track and field paths with some steeply rising ground to give the heart and lungs some exercise.
Map. OS Explorer 223 Northampton & Market Harborough
Starting point: Beside the road near the Tollemache Arms. GR 776803
How to get there: Harrington lies just north of the A14 between junctions 2 and 3. At junction 2, turn north onto the A508 and at Kelmarsh turn right to Harrington.
Refreshments: The Tollemache Arms. Telephone: 01536 710469.

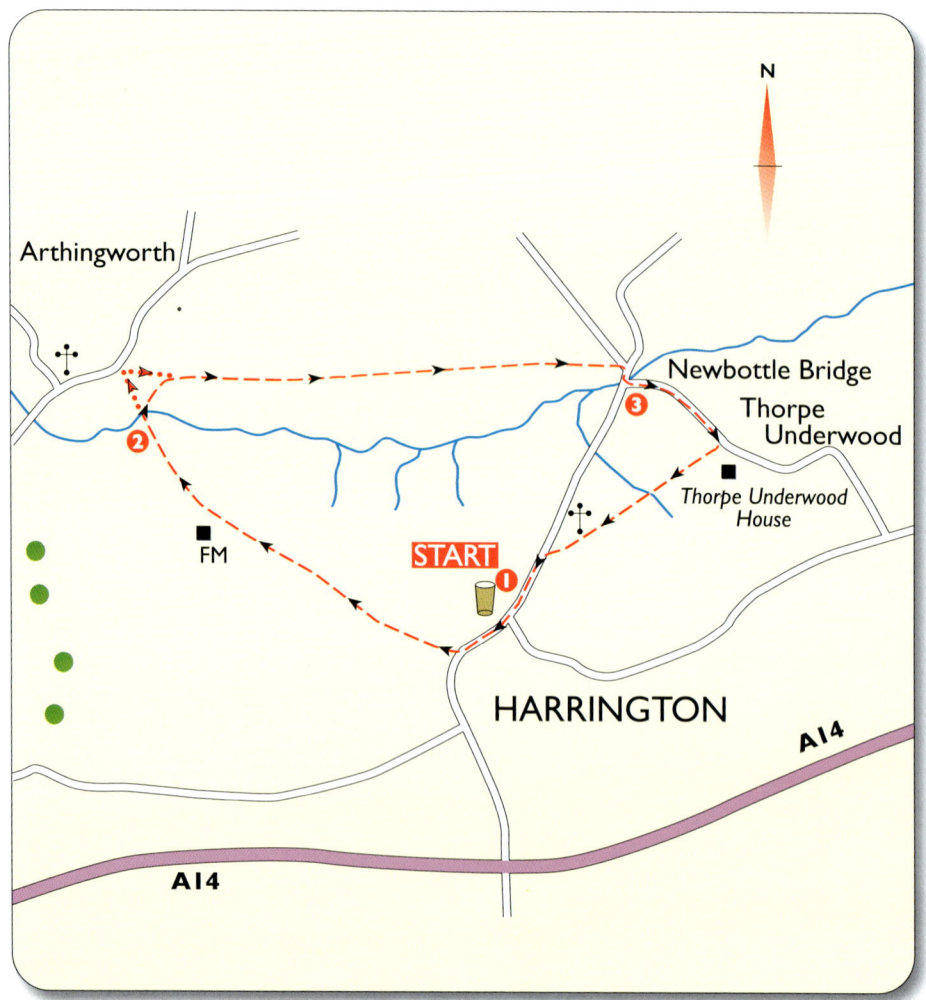

a telegraph pole on the horizon trying to keep a good pace; the terrain then levels out for a long stretch. This is a quiet and peaceful area of open countryside punctuated with birdsong. Two large metal gates give onto the road. Turn right here towards **Newbottle Bridge**.

3 Cross the bridge and turn left signed to **Thorpe Underwood**. Carry on up this fairly steep hill until, at the top, a footpath sign leads to what looks like an impregnable gate! Fear not – the entry phone is for the large gate, the other beside it can be opened by reaching over to pull back a spring. There

■ *The bridge over the ford* ■

are a few wooden rails to the right which can be climbed if necessary. Head for the waymarker into the field which you cross in the direction of a pylon. Follow down the slope going right to a wooden footbridge beside some oak trees and some newly-planted trees. Another steep climb up to the church awaits. Enter the churchyard via a very low stile and leave on the other side of the church. Turn left along the footpath leading back into **Harrington**.

17 Deene

An Estate Village Delight

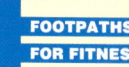

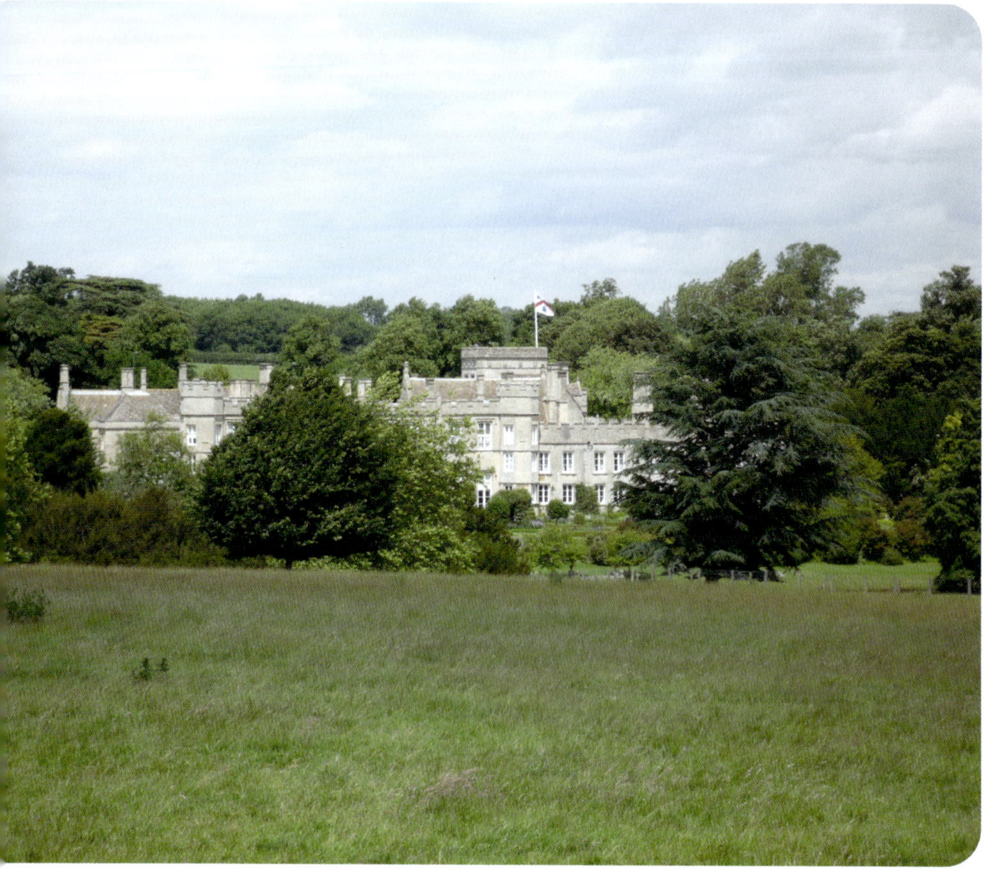

The grand mansion in Deene Park

The village of Deene is small, with the imposing mansion of Deene Park in its midst. Built in the 16th century, it has been the home of the Brudenell family since 1514 and was the seat of the Earls of Cardigan. The 7th Earl led the Charge of the Light Brigade at Balaclava in1854. The walk is full of variety going as it does out into open fields, through woodland, and into the interesting village of Deenethorpe before returning via the lovely lake to the start.

1 Leave the village hall and turn left along the road with the high brick wall on the right. Soon after passing the main entrance to **Deene Park**, go through a wooden gate onto a track which will lead through the churchyard and out through a gate to an area which can be a bit muddy. You are now walking behind the dam with the lake at eye level. Carry on to the wooden bridge which goes over the rushing weir then proceed uphill, with a lovely row of horse chestnut trees on the right, and onto the road. Cross with great care and turn left. Take the bridleway sign leading off right and walk uphill with the hedge on your left. Now's the time to test your fitness! Between little bursts of speed, take it slow and steady, but do keep going because the gradient is not steep. Ignore waymarker signs and carry on ahead on the track through the open fields, ultimately heading for a coppice called **Burn Coppice** and some buildings. The track goes on following the contours of the wood and then swings away left towards **Forest Lodge**. At these dilapidated buildings, turn right along the obvious track going slightly uphill into the distance with the hedge on the left and another opportunity to get up a head of steam. On reaching some more buildings turn right. Go ahead at the metal barrier to join **Benefield Road**.

2 Turn right and after a couple of hundred yards, turn left through a metal gate, almost beside a white-painted hydrant, into a large field with woodland on the right. After a considerable distance following the contours of the wood, turn right at a very obvious break in the fence and a waymarker. Climb the stile into the woods swinging round left with the

GRADE: 2
ESTIMATED CALORIE BURN: 780

Distance: 5½ miles
Time: 3 hours
Stiles: 4
Terrain: Mostly firm underfoot though there are a few areas which can be muddy at times. There are some long gradual slopes uphill
Map: OS Explorer 224 Corby, Kettering & Wellingborough
Starting point: The village hall, Deene. GR 948928
How to get there: Deene is well signed off the A43 north-east of Corby. Turn into the village passing the gates of Deene Park and continue to the first building on the right which is the village hall.
Refreshments: The Queens Head in Bulwick. Telephone 01780 450272.

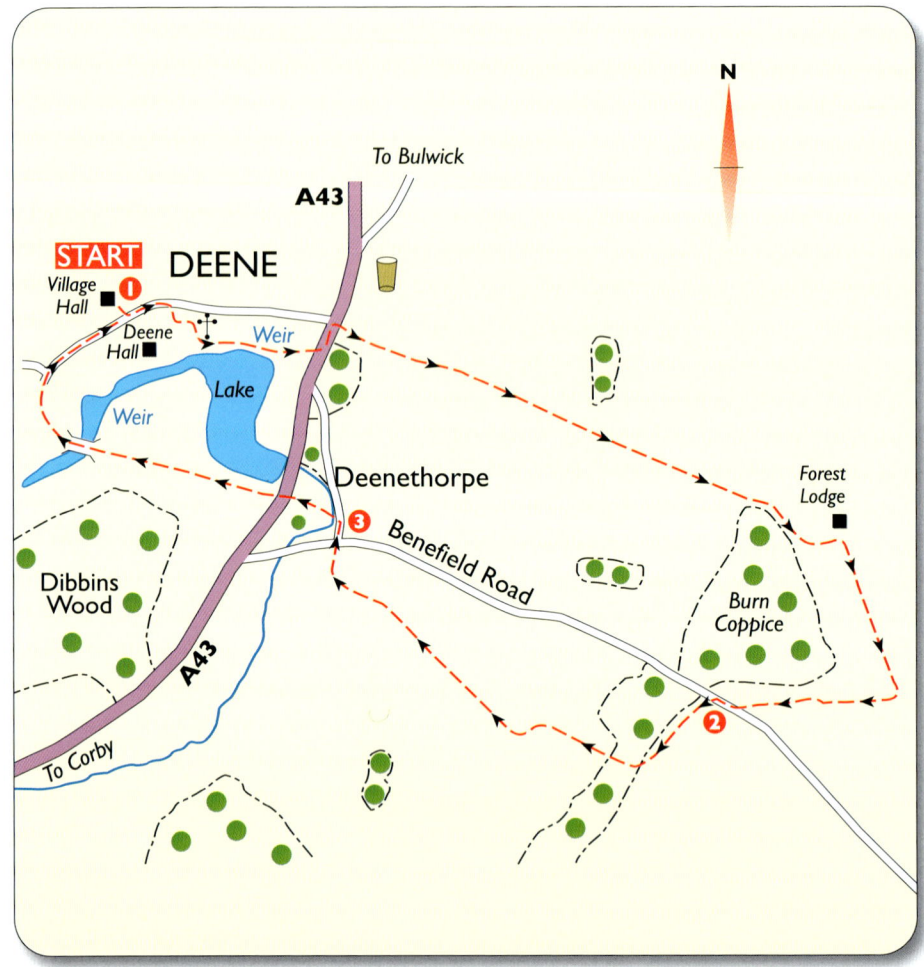

wide path and a view of the open fields framed with trees at the end. Enter this field and veer left with the hedge on the left. Notice a ladder and what appears to be a large armchair in an ash tree in the hedge. This is not for your comfort even if you could reach it over the deep ditch! Continue uphill towards an array of mobile phone masts and onto a disused concrete runway. Here is a chance to break into a gentle trot as you head right towards the windsock. On reaching it, turn left. About 100 yards further along, yellow waymarkers point right. Take the left-hand track going downhill towards some houses in the village of **Deenethorpe** and go through the kissing gate onto the road.

■ *Water lilies on the lake* ■

3 Turn down right to join another road. Go straight across passing a telephone box and a letter box. Continue on downhill past lovely houses and turn left over a bridge with white railings at the bottom. Soon you will meet the A43. Cross over into the spinney opposite. Something of a pioneering spirit may be needed here in the height of summer when the undergrowth is very lush! Keep to the left-hand side heading in the direction of woodland. There is a waymarker in the middle marking a wooden plank which goes over a deep-set stream. A welcome footpath sign will lead you into the woods through which you meander and then climb the stile into a field. A waymarker points straight ahead up the hill which will give the heart a bit of exercise but you will get your reward at the top when **Deene Park** and the lake come into view. Carry on straight ahead keeping a little fenced spinney of trees on your right. At the bottom is another view of the lake and a track. Go towards the hedge on the right where there is a waymarker. Climb the stile, go down a flight of steps and across a wooden footbridge to another stile and emerge onto a track. Turn right over a cattle grid and, keeping sheep pens on the right go down to the road back into the village and turn right to the starting point.

18 Badby

Pretty as a Picture

![Crossing a buttercup meadow]

■ *Crossing a buttercup meadow* ■

The name Badby originates from the Anglo-Saxon Badden Burh which was a fortified site on Arbury Hill, the county's highest point at 217 metres and which is thought to have been the centre of a royal estate. Badby Wood is famous for its bluebells which are a sight to behold in the spring. Badby is also the start of the long-distance Nene Way footpath so your ultimate challenge could be to walk its length (in sections, of course!).

This lovely circuit is full of contrast going as it does through meadows and woodland with beautiful views over the gentle Northamptonshire countryside, as well as visiting some pretty villages.

1 Walk down **Court Yard Lane** opposite the **Maltsers pub** and carry on to the end. Here you will encounter **Nene Way** signs which you follow to the village of **Newnham** past a couple of wooden sculptures. On reaching a large gate at a corner of a field go onto the road into **Newnham**, turning right. Walk up the long hill trying to keep a good pace through this attractive village. Just before reaching the church with its unusual open tower, turn down **Manor Lane** on the right passing a row of fascinating stone cottages and a nuttery owned by the Woodland Trust. Continue along the 'No Through Road' and then follow the **Nene Way** sign to the left and over the grassy hill where cattle often graze. Follow the white discs which are attached to the stiles and gates, at one point getting a glimpse on the left of **Everdon Hall**, a manor house built in 1690. This cluster of cottages is called **Little Everdon**. The sign leading to the road is a little difficult to see but it is under a spreading chestnut tree in front of a stone cottage.

2 Join the road and walk right with a stone wall on the right. Cross the road, now leaving the **Nene Way**, and walk on the raised pathway which will

GRADE: 3
ESTIMATED CALORIE BURN: 800?

Distance: 6½ miles
Time: 3 hours
Stiles: 4
Terrain: Mostly undulating but with some steep slopes to test your level of fitness.
Map: OS Explorer 206 Edge Hill & Fenny Compton
Starting point: Beside the road near the Maltsers Country Inn. GR 558593
How to get there: Badby is 3 miles south of Daventry, just off the A361 road to Banbury. Coming in from the north, take the second turning into the village. The Maltsers Country Inn is on the right.
Refreshments: The Maltsers Country Inn in Badby. Telephone: 01327 702905.

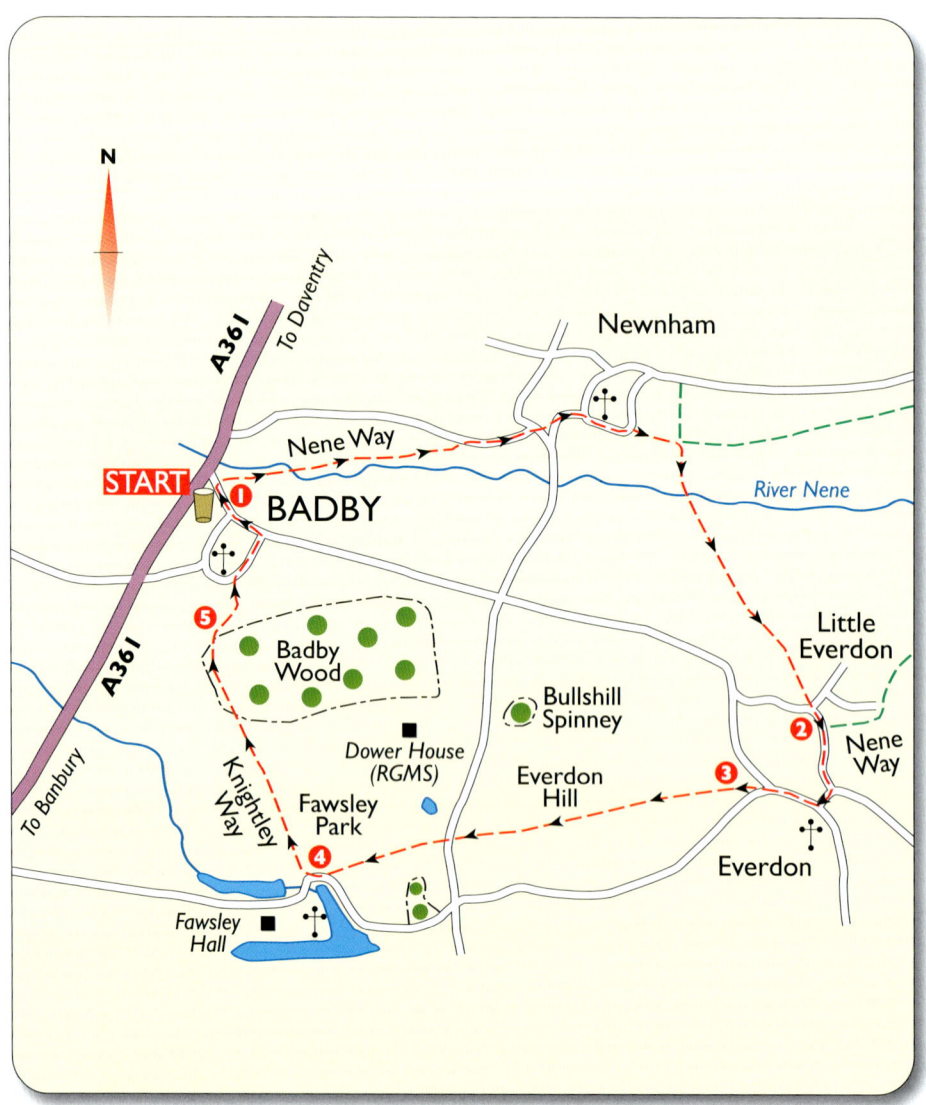

take you to **Everdon**. Turn right and follow the road round and right in front of the church continuing along the main street.

3 Where the road swings round right, keep left signed to **Fawsley**. Very soon, take the footpath off to the right beside a yellow salt box and go over a stile and into a field. Continue up the hill at a slow but steady pace and your

■ *Wooden sculptures seen along the way* ■

reward will be a wonderful view. From now on, follow the waymarkers across several fields, soon aiming for a telecommunications tower (resembling a lighthouse). After passing a farm, continue to the road which you cross, going through another metal gate and up the field in front of you. Keeping the fence on the left, cross the next large field keeping that tower slightly on the right. If you look over to the left, you catch a glimpse of **Little Fawsley church** and, further along, the lake.

4 On reaching the road turn right towards a gravelled area used for parking. You now embark on the **Knightley Way** which leads out of the car park. The way is well marked with round white discs. The first hill you encounter is long and certainly going to make you puff but remember the maxim to keep a slow and steady pace, only allowing yourself to stop at the top, then turn round, and reap the reward of a wonderful panorama. When your pulse rate returns to normal, walk on to the tranquillity of **Badby Wood** which is carpeted with bluebells in springtime.

5 When you emerge from the wood, cross a grassy field and enter a narrow track leading downhill at first and then steeply uphill to **Badby**. You may now congratulate yourself on completing this hike!

■ *A wisteria covered house in Newnham* ■

Fermyn Woods

Red Kite Land

■ *The Skylarks café* ■

Fermyn Woods Country Park is a delightful area full of trails with many nature notes which children as well as adults will enjoy. It is also the start of the Lyveden Way which is a long-distance path of approximately 10 miles that goes out to Lyveden New Bield and Wadenhoe before returning to the park. Lyveden New Bield now in the care of the National Trust contains the shell of a very elegant cruciform house that was to have been the home of Thomas Tresham. His family was implicated in the Gunpowder Plot, however, and he spent most of his life in prison for his Catholic faith so the house was never completed.

GRADE: 3
ESTIMATED CALORIE BURN: 800

Distance: 6¼ miles
Time: 3 hours
Stiles: 4
Terrain: Easy going on the flat through fields and woodland
Map: OS Explorer 224 Corby, Kettering & Wellingborough
Starting point: The car park at Fermyn Woods Country Park (fee payable). GR 954849
How to get there: The country park is well signed off the A6116 Corby to Thrapston road near Brigstock.
Refreshments: The Skylark Café near the car park. Open all year, times may vary. Telephone: 01536 373625.

This walk leaves the park and heads out across fields and through woodland giving ample opportunity to get up a head of steam!

1 Leave the car park walking to the other side of a large children's play area passing a few picnic tables and smaller play area on the right, and up to an obvious gravel path going towards the trees. Walk uphill on the path continuing until you reach a disabled parking clearing. About 20 yards further on, turn right over a wooden footbridge into a field.

2 Keeping the woods on your left continue up and round the margin of the field, glancing back at the lovely panorama. Ignore tracks and paths into the wood and turn left at the top still keeping the hedge on the left. Carry on again round the field into a dip and up the slope where at the top you will see a **Lyveden Way** sign directing you left through the hedge and then left along the field with the woods on the left. After a considerable distance and walking with pace, you will see another **Lyveden Way** sign and 5 yards further on, a bridleway marker into the woods. Ignore this and carry on until round the next bend. The **Lyveden Way** marker goes forward right but you leave it and enter the woods on a bridleway. A fenced-off area can be seen on the left. Carry on in this quiet area and where the path swings left, go straight ahead by the marker post onto a smaller track. The path ahead can be a bit boggy but with sidesteps here and there it can be dodged. Where a bridleway marker goes right, ignore it and go straight ahead and then round to the right.

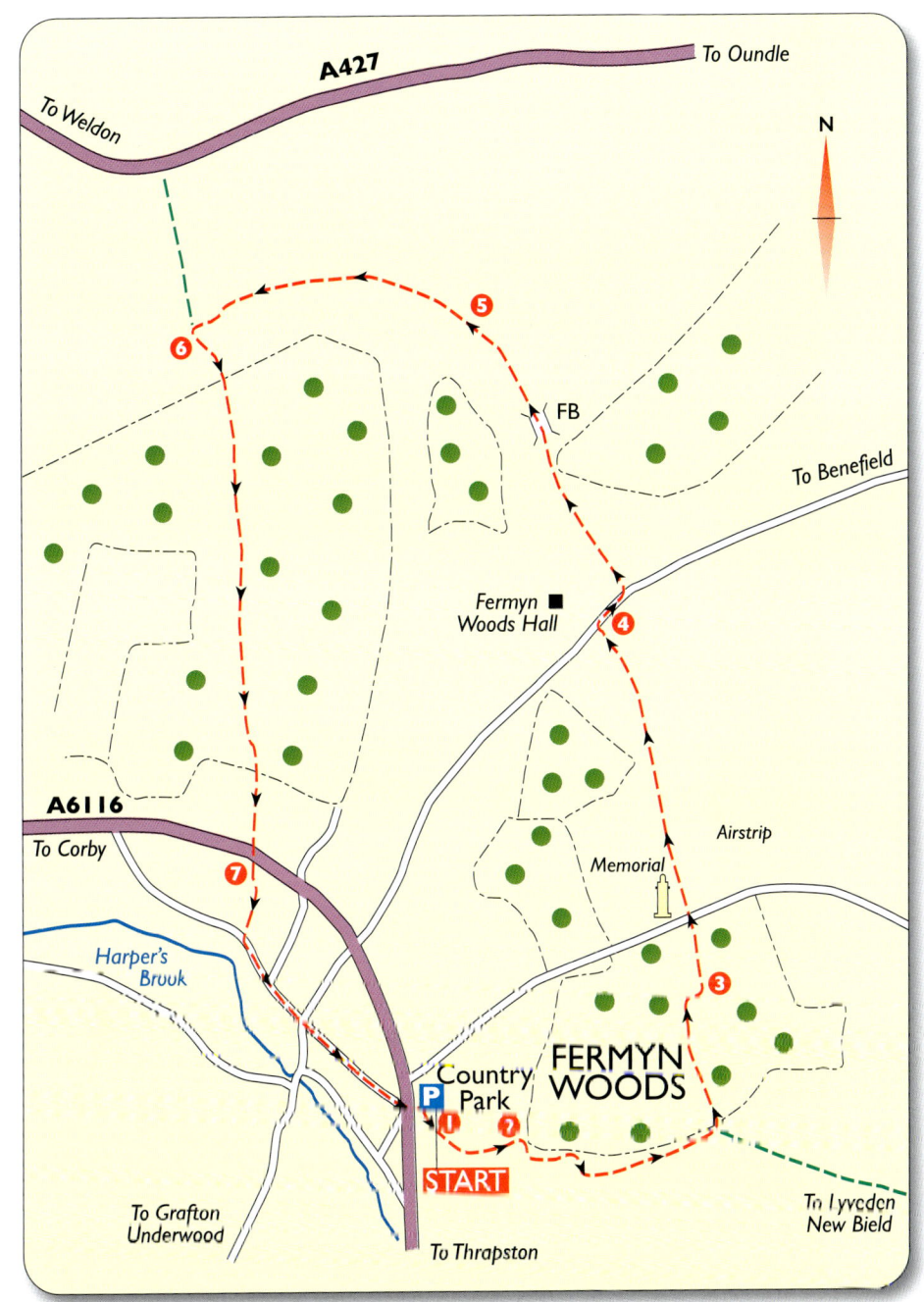

To Weldon

A427

To Oundle

N

5

FB

6

To Benefield

Fermyn ■
Woods Hall

4

A6116

To Corby

Airstrip

Memorial

7

3

Harper's
Brook

**FERMYN
WOODS**

P Country
Park

1

2

START

To Grafton
Underwood

To Thrapston

To Lyveden
New Bield

■ *Deep in the countryside* ■

3 Turn left at a marker leading to the road which you cross.

4 Go through the white gates beside the memorial and along the track to an obvious footbridge leading into a field. The 'going' has been a bit soft up until now so here's a chance to stride out a bit and up the heart rate. Red kites are often seen here wheeling in the sky. Veer left to the hedge and carry on to a metal gate onto the road near **Fermyn Woods Hall** which has its origins in the 14th century and which now offers bed and breakfast accommodation. The Brigstock horse trials are held here. Turn right.

5 After approximately 250 yards, turn left at the bridleway sign down a farm road. Turn right at the sixth telegraph pole to the left-hand corner of the trees and continue ahead along the field edge with the hedge on the left passing a pond and going over a footbridge.

6 At the corner of the third field bear left, then right, walking along the wide grassy path on the right-hand side of the field. Go through the boundary and continue to walk through the long narrow field to a metal gate. Turn left down the track, past a metal barrier, and into **Fermyn Woods**. Carry on for approximately 1 mile. As the track starts to bear left downhill, go right at the marker onto a broad grassy track. Bear left down a slope and pass right through a gap in the hedge a few yards beyond the marker. Continue ahead to a stile to the right of the telegraph pole. Proceed across the field to a stile and footbridge. Cross the road to a stile on the other side.

7 The footpath sign is very misleading in its direction so cross the field going diagonally left towards a stile in the hedge opposite, beside a red shed and some leylandii. Follow the path to the road, at which point turn left into **Brigstock**. Carry on along the road and bear left down **Stable Hill**. Keep going straight along the road for some distance, putting a bit of pace in your step, between houses and, where the road swings right, you will see a flight of steps on the left taking you up and over the footbridge back to the country park. Turn right back to the start.

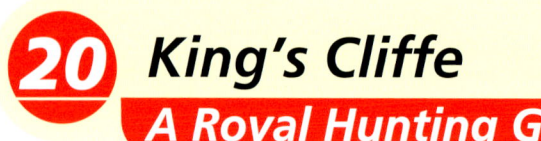

20 King's Cliffe

A Royal Hunting Ground

FOOTPATHS FOR FITNES

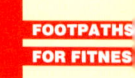

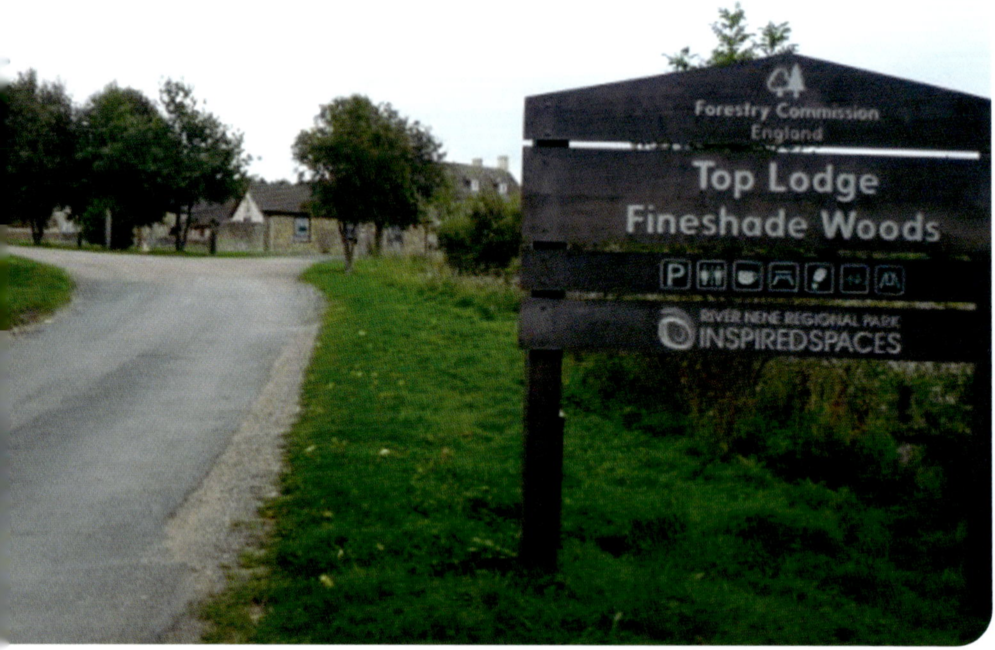

Top Lodge at the end of point 1 of the route

This is a delightful village full of lovely stone cottages to rival those of the Cotswolds. Together with neighbouring villages, it once sat among the trees of Rockingham Forest, a good hunting ground for kings. The abundance of wood made the local population famous for its wood turning and it is said that, for a wager, a turner made 417 egg cups in eight hours! One of King's Cliffe's sons was William Law, born in 1685, who raised money for the poor. Beggars would flock to the village and the vicar and the locals complained that Law was the cause of 'miserable poverty of the parish'. An anonymous stranger gave him £1,000 with which he founded a school for girls.

The walk goes along the main street before joining the track which leads into Fineshade Woods. It leaves the woods going through fields and beside Blatherwycke Lake before returning to King's Cliffe.

1 With the church on your left, walk up to **West Street** and turn left in front of the **Cross Keys pub**. Carry on along this attractive road with its pretty cottages until the road junction where you cross the road and continue up **Wood Lane**. Turn left with the bridleway sign and go ahead passing a woodyard on the right and then through the gap beside a metal gate fortified with lumps of concrete. Carry on following the **Jurassic Way** signs into **Westhay Wood** still keeping straight ahead. Keep your eye on the skies here and you are quite likely to see red kites, with their distinctive forked tails, wheeling around. The track swings round to the right after **Smelter's Walk** and shortly after this you emerge from the wood onto a tarmac lane where there is a good chance to gather speed if you haven't already done so. Soon you will arrive at **Top Lodge** on your right with its café, craft shop and the opportunity to learn about the work of the RSPB.

2 When you are refreshed, carry on downhill and turn left immediately after crossing the bridge over the disused railway. Climb the stile into the field and go straight ahead on the obvious track to the wood opposite. Walk through the wood and climb the stile into a field where you go straight ahead with

GRADE: 3
ESTIMATED CALORIE BURN: 1200

Distance: 7½ miles
Time: 4 hours
Stiles: 14
Terrain: Mostly firm underfoot, with a few gentle slopes.
Map: OS Explorer 224 Corby, Kettering and Wellingborough
Starting point: Outside the church in King's Cliffe. GR 007972
How to get there: Leave the A43 Corby–Stamford road near Deene Park, signed to Bulwick, Blatherwycke and King's Cliffe. In King's Cliffe turn down the small lane opposite the Cross Keys pub and park near the church.
Refreshments: The Cross Keys pub in King's Cliffe (telephone: 01780 470276) or the Lodge Cafe in Fineshade Woods which is open 10 am to 5 pm every day except Christmas Day.

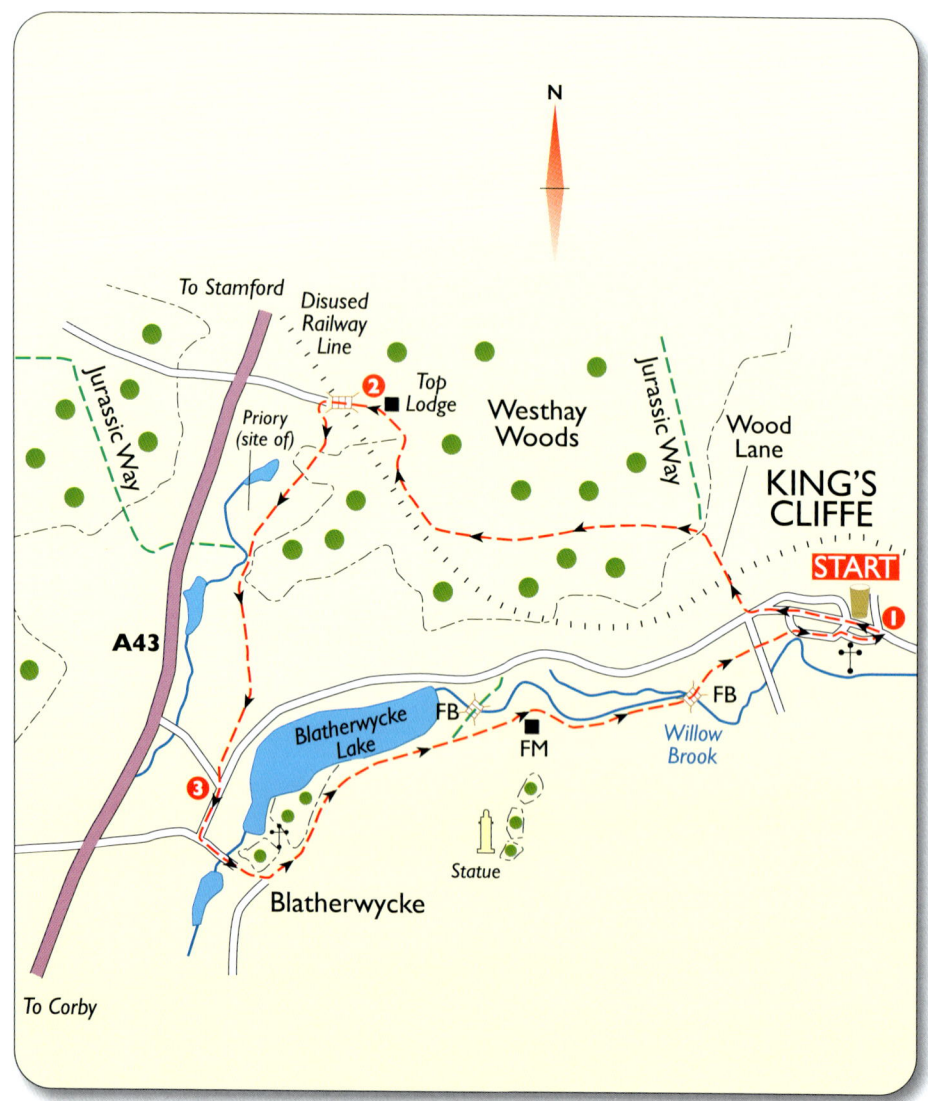

a view of a lake and an imposing mansion on the shore. Continue uphill with a wire fence on the right and follow the waymarker, going over a stile onto a narrow enclosed path with the converted stable block down on the right. Climb the next stile and proceed diagonally left downhill towards the iron railings of a concrete bridge. Here you leave the **Jurassic Way**. Instead of turning right, carry on through metal gates with a stream on the right.

Fancy meeting you here!

Within yards, strike off uphill towards the end of the woods and then aim between two telegraph poles but nearer the one on the left. Climb the stile by the metal gate into the field and notice the gates of **Laxton Hall** over to the right. Climb the next stile and go straight ahead keeping the hedge on your right. At a gap in the hedge turn right and then left with the sign, leaving the hedge going diagonally through the centre of the field heading just to the left of a large oak tree. Just before reaching the tree, carry on down to waymarker signs at the end of the hedge on the right. At this point, turn right keeping the hedge on the right and walking parallel with **Blatherwycke Lake** at the bottom of the hill. Continue ahead climbing two more stiles heading towards farm buildings until you arrive at the road junction ¼ mile outside the village of **Blatherwycke**.

3 Walk ahead into the village crossing a delightful area at the bridge and passing the entrance to what was **Blatherwycke Hall**. Turn left with the waymarker in front of a converted barn opposite a cottage, No 23. Your route now is straight ahead for a considerable distance passing **Blatherwyck church** tucked away in the trees on the left. Over to the right you will notice a classical statue standing somewhat incongruously in the middle of the field! Nobody seems to know why it is there but it has been suggested that it once stood in the grounds of the Hall. Eventually you can go no further, as indicated by a sign saying 'Private Property'. At this point turn left as indicated through the gap in the hedge and immediately right beside the hedge. Where the hedge ends, carry on ahead towards some farm buildings. Go through the farm buildings to a marker in the fence on the left and carry on as indicated by the signs, crossing innumerable stiles and a wooden footbridge eventually arriving at the allotments in **King's Cliffe**. Follow along the bottom of the allotments before emerging onto the gravelled road where you go straight ahead to meet **Maltings Lane**. Here turn right, going between stone walls, to arrive at the church.

Calorie Chart

The following chart shows the approximate calories spent per hour by a person weighing 8 stone (112 lbs), 11 stone (154 lbs) and 15 stone (210 lbs)

	8 stone	11 stone	15 stone
Walking, 2 mph	160	240	312
Walking, 3 mph	210	320	416

Note that these figures are based on moderate, not vigorous, activity.

Other Northamptonshire titles from Countryside Books

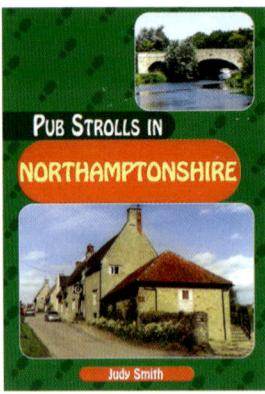

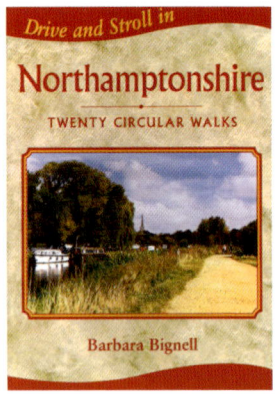

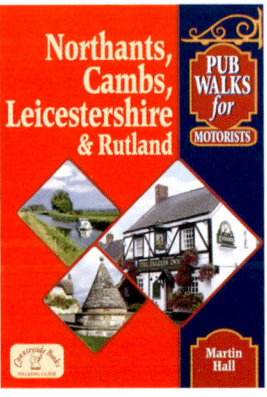

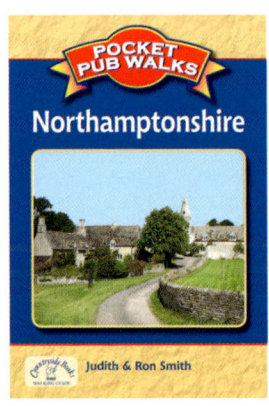